SpringerBriefs in Computer Science

Series Editors
Stan Zdonik
Peng Ning
Shashi Shekhar
Jonathan Katz
Xindong Wu
Lakhmi C. Jain
David Padua
Xuemin (Sherman) Shen
Borko Furht
V.S. Subrahmanian
Martial Hebert
Katsushi Ikeuchi
Bruno Siciliano

T0214292

For further volumes:
http://www.springer.com/series/10028

Rafael Grompone von Gioi

A Contrario
Line Segment Detection

 Springer

Rafael Grompone von Gioi
CMLA, ENS Cachan
Cachan, France

ISSN 2191-5768   ISSN 2191-5776 (electronic)
ISBN 978-1-4939-0574-4   ISBN 978-1-4939-0575-1 (eBook)
DOI 10.1007/978-1-4939-0575-1
Springer New York Heidelberg Dordrecht London

Library of Congress Control Number: 2014931770

Printed on acid-free paper

Springer is part of Springer Science+Business Media (www.springer.com)

Preface

Among the myriad algorithms and techniques that constitute the field of computer vision, this work focuses on just one: the LSD algorithm for line segment detection in digital images. The interest in this algorithm is twofold: First, due to its relative simplicity, the method can be understood in full detail and provides a complete example of a low-level image analysis algorithm. Second, the method is based on the *a contrario* approach and it illustrates well the kind of parameterless algorithms of this family. In practice, the method produces fairly good results, comparable to the state-of-the-art methods and without human intervention. The reader is invited to try out the online demo of the algorithm on new images and to explore the companion archive of experiments, both of them available at the IPOL journal's website [36]. A good experiment is worth a thousand words.

The introductory chapter (Chap. 1) presents the general principles underlying the design of the algorithm. Chapter 2 briefly introduces the *a contrario* approach and then concentrates on the application of this framework to the problem of line segment detection. The LSD algorithm is described in Chap. 3 and its behavior is discussed in Chap. 4. The final chapter (Chap. 5) considers the limitations of the method and points to the possible improvements and extensions.

The research reported here was performed in collaboration with Jérémie Jakubowicz, Jean-Michel Morel, and Gregory Randall, while I was pursuing the Ph.D. degree. I certainly learned much from them and would like to thank them for their patience, generosity, and guidance.

I am indebted to many collaborators and friends for their comments and suggestions that greatly improved this text. Viorica Pătrăucean read the whole manuscript in detail, proposing countless corrections and improvements. Mauricio Delbracio, Gabriele Facciolo, Carolina Gazzaneo, Jérémie Jakubowicz, Enric Meinhardt-Llopis, Jean-Michel Morel, Gregory Randall, and Rodrigo Verschae also read the manuscript, or part of it, providing valuable feedback. I am grateful to each of them.

Paris, France
June 2013

Rafael Grompone von Gioi

Contents

Chapter 1
Introduction

The aim of image analysis is to extract useful information from digital images. The fundamental problem lies in how to combine the information from multiple measurements, the pixel values, into a coherent interpretation. This work discusses a very reduced version of this general problem, namely the detection of *line segments*.

In our context, line segments are locally straight image edges; that is, sharp transitions of image brightness that follow locally a straight line. Figure 1.1 shows some examples. This description is enough to get an intuitive understanding of the concept. A precise definition implies a corresponding detecting algorithm; inversely, an algorithm implicitly provides a definition of image line segments. As we will see, every known algorithm for line segment detection has shortcomings and a fully satisfactory one is yet to be proposed. As a consequence, we will have to rely on future developments for a precise definition that is consistent with the intuitive notion of a line segment.

Fig. 1.1 An image and the line segments detected by LSD

R. Grompone von Gioi, *A Contrario Line Segment Detection*, SpringerBriefs in Computer Science, DOI 10.1007/978-1-4939-0575-1_1, © The Author(s) 2014

The detection of line segments is a classic problem in computer vision and numerous algorithms have been proposed, each with its own advantages and disadvantages. Among them, this book concentrates on one named LSD, an acronym[1] for Line Segment Detector [35, 36]. The present chapter contains a philosophical statement of the design criteria used in LSD, describing the strategies in general terms; the algorithm itself will be described in the following chapters.

LSD can be characterized as a fast and parameterless algorithm. While it is easy to understand the advantages of a fast algorithm, the strategy used to obtain it deserves a brief discussion. The idea is simple and well known: to divide the task into two steps, a search for candidates followed by a validation of the good ones. A smart heuristic search may result in an efficient method by reducing the number of candidates to test, ideally including all the relevant ones. The validation step must provide a conclusive decision about the presence or not of the sought structure. More on this in the next section.

The parameterless aspect merits a more attentive discussion. An important aspect of LSD is the fact that it is fully automatic. That is, it can be used without the need for parameter tuning. To this aim, the algorithm was carefully designed so that every step performs reasonably well without human intervention and for a large spectrum of images. LSD is not perfect, of course, but it shows that it is possible to perform automatic image analysis to some extent. The meaning and interest of parameterless methods are discussed in Sect. 1.2. The cornerstone of the family of parameterless algorithms presented here is the non-accidentalness principle that will be introduced in Sect. 1.3. In a nutshell, an observed structure is relevant if it would rarely occur by chance.

1.1 Heuristic Search Plus Validation

There are several kinds of computational solutions that can be proposed for a problem. Ideally, the problem can be formulated into a well-founded theory where the optimal solution is deduced with an efficient algorithm to compute it. Unfortunately, this is not always the case; the exact solution may be unknown or its complexity could lead to a computational burden.

A long-standing problem in science is the decomposition of integer numbers into their prime factors [49]. The problem is well defined and has been studied for centuries. Despite this, no known algorithm is able to solve the general case efficiently. As numbers become large, the quantity of operations required to perform the factorization increases drastically, demanding prohibitive computational time and rendering the task impractical even for the fastest computers. It is unknown whether this is an insurmountable limit, but it is widely accepted that the intrinsic complexity of the problem precludes the existence of an efficient algorithm. The security of many current cryptographic methods relies on this fact, illustrating how strong this belief has become.

---

[1] I am grateful to Gabriele Facciolo for suggesting this name. The name hides a reference to the song *Lucy in the Sky with Diamonds* by the Beatles.

In some problems, efficient algorithms for *verifying* a proposed solution are known. In lack of an efficient algorithm to *find* the solution, the *heuristic search plus validation* approach can be tried: a heuristic is used to propose potential solutions which are then validated or not by the verification method. This approach does not guarantee finding a solution, but when found, it is a correct one. The *efficiency* of the verification method is essential, otherwise there is not much gain from the approach. This strategy is well known in computer science [65].

In the factorization problem described before, it is easy to verify a proposed solution: the multiplication of the factors $p_1 p_2 \cdots p_n$ should be equal to the number to be factorized and each p_i should be prime (this can be done in polynomial time [2]). Given these conditions, one can exploit some regularities to obtain a fast solution for some numbers; as a trivial example, 2 is an obvious factor of even numbers. Unfortunately, the speedup in this case is effective only for a small proportion of numbers. This is a huge simplification used only to illustrate the idea, see [49] for an appropriate discussion.

Images and visual structures are complex. Consider line segments: there are N^4 possible line segments with integer end points in an $N \times N$ image. In this case the space of possible candidates is not huge; still, an exhaustive search leads to a computational burden. Consider now the visual scenes in natural human environments. Imagine the number of different shapes and the number of different familiar objects; the explosion in a variety of points of view and scales leads to a gigantic configuration's space. It is unthinkable to explore even a tiny fraction of it.

Fortunately, natural images are highly redundant and structures are highly regular. For example, when part of a line segment is found, the full structure can be deduced or gradually guessed from it. Efficient heuristics can exploit these regularities. While hardly enough to lead to an optimal solution, it seems feasible to design smart heuristics and justified validation steps that provide appropriate solutions for many cases. The price to pay for good realizable algorithms is, probably, accepting occasional failures.

It is suggested in [30] that the human visual system is confronted with similar obstacles. According to this view, the aim of perception is to find a configuration

Fig. 1.2 What do you see? (Picture by Ronald C. James)

of the known world compatible with the sensory information. But the space of possible configurations that an adult human should consider is colossal; heuristics are needed to reduce the search. It is also suggested that the laws of perceptual grouping described by the Gestalt School [62] are part of these heuristics. Occasionally, the visual system fails to make sense of a scene. Figure 1.2 shows an example: when people see this image for the first time, they usually see just a bunch of black blobs, at least for a while. But if hinted that a Dalmatian dog is present, it is usually easy to see it. In other words, the heuristics initially failed; but when the right hypothesis is tested it is immediately validated.

As the problems handled by computer vision grow in complexity, the discipline will be confronted more and more often with this explosion of configurations; the only direction for a breakthrough out of very simple problems may be the heuristic search plus validation approach.

> *if a machine is expected to be infallible, it cannot also be intelligent.*
> *There are several mathematical theorems which say almost exactly*
> *that. But these theorems say nothing about how much intelligence*
> *may be displayed if a machine makes no pretence at infallibility.*
> Alan Turing, "Lecture on the Automatic Computing Engine" [17, p. 394]

1.2 Parameterless Algorithms

An algorithm is a precisely defined procedure to solve a task in a finite number of steps [48]. The usually accepted formal definition is due to Alan Turing and his Turing Machines [63, 81]; simply stated, an algorithm is a method that can be translated into a computer program written in a general-purpose programming language. Everything must be rigorously and unambiguously specified so it can be translated into a computer program. A classic example is Euclid's algorithm for computing the greatest common divisor of two natural numbers.

Algorithms often work on some input data to produce some output data. In Euclid's algorithm the input data are the two numbers and the output is a third number, the greatest common divisor. An algorithm can also require parameters: that is, additional inputs to control how some aspect of the main task is carried out. For example, an algorithm to compute the square root of a number could take a parameter to specify the number of digits required in the decimal expansion of the result. Strictly speaking, parameters are part of the input; whether an input is considered a parameter or not is a question of interpretation, it depends on what is the main task of the algorithm, which are necessary inputs, and which are optional modifiers.

Image processing and computer vision are carried out by algorithms. A simple example is an algorithm for smoothing an image by filtering it with a Gaussian kernel. The input is an image, the output is the filtered image, and a parameter σ is necessary to specify the standard deviation of the Gaussian kernel. The main task is to smooth the input image and the parameter σ gives some control on the desired smoothness.

The ability to control an algorithm through parameters can be very useful when an image is being interactively modified by a user: one can manually fiddle with the parameters to produce the best result in visual terms. In such a case, the algorithm becomes a digital tool for humans to craft the desired result.

A parametric algorithm may also be useful when a visual task needs to be solved automatically by a machine. In some problems the *a priori* information available is enough to specify correctly all the parameters. For example, under controlled camera, lighting, and exposure conditions, the noise level of an image may be known in advance, allowing to set the amount of filtering required to remove it. Alternatively, in hierarchical systems, a high level task may be able to dynamically adjust lower level parameters to obtain the best result. In both cases it is a good thing to be able to adapt the algorithm to the situation in particular.

Yet, this is far from covering all cases. Hierarchical systems often work feedfordwardly and no further information is available at higher levels of the chain. A pervasive example is the use of the Canny algorithm [14] to provide edge points: although Canny's method depends on three parameters, algorithms built on it usually take the edge map as input without controlling its parameter, which are just fixed to arbitrary values. There are relatively few discussions in the literature on how to set these parameters and in practice they are usually manually tuned. It is, however, not always simple for human users to set parameters manually, especially when three or more are involved. The need for manual tuning is often an unavoidable nuisance resulting from the absence of automatic algorithms producing good results. The reason why parameterless algorithms are uncommon is that image processing and computer vision problems are extremely challenging, and producing fairly good automatic algorithms is very hard.

Consider the following formula [11], discovered by Ramanujan and published in 1914, which can be used to build an efficient algorithm for computing approximations to π:

$$\frac{1}{\pi} = \frac{\sqrt{8}}{9801} \sum_{n=0}^{\infty} \frac{(4n)!}{(n!)^4} \frac{1103 + 26390n}{396^{4n}} .$$

There are some fixed numbers in it: 9801, 1103, 26390, and 396. Should we consider these numbers as parameters of the derived algorithm? Of course not. The algorithm would change its meaning if these values were changed. Ramanujan could have provided the formula with undefined constants, arguing that it is valid for some values. But he also took the trouble to find these values, which is not trivial as shown in [11]. These numbers are part of Ramanujan's contribution.

The point is that a numerical constant is not necessarily a parameter. Nonetheless, it is a common practice in computer vision and image processing to consider any number in an algorithm as a parameter and try to modify its value to see the results. Indeed, the results of many algorithms in the field improve significantly by tuning the parameters for a particular data set. Far from perfection, this is an undesirable situation.

Making an algorithm parametric or parameterless is a choice of the designer; it is the choice between two different cases of use. A parameterless algorithm must produce the result automatically, making all the required decisions based only on the input; a parametric algorithm gives some control to adjust the result. One aims at "out-of-the-box use" while the other requires "expert users".

A parameterless method is not necessarily as Ramanujan's formula, which gives the exact result. An approximate and automatic solution can be better than a exact one requiring manual tuning. It depends, of course, on the use. A good parameterless algorithm should produce reasonable results for a wide range of data without parameter tuning. It constitutes a risky statement for a designer to propose a parameterless algorithm, as this implies assuming the responsibility for possible bad results without the reassuring refuge given by parameter tuning to improve them.

Any method can be rendered parameterless by fixing the parameter values; but this only makes sense when it can still produce useful results. A good parametric algorithm may become useless in the process. Inversely, a parameterless method may rely on fixed numeric quantities and in such case their values must be carefully selected, becoming part of the design. Once fixed, these quantities are not parameters in the sense of being "knobs" available for adjusting the algorithm's behavior.

Finally, a parameterless algorithm can be modified. One can study its internal workings and then propose variations. In the case of Ramanujan's formula, a faster convergence may be envisaged; understanding how the approximation to π is obtained, one may find a better formula using similar techniques. In the same way, a computer vision algorithm could be improved by changing part of the algorithm or by modifying internal numerical quantities for a particular case. (The latter is hardly possible for Ramanujan's formula.) This amounts to proposing a new method, related but different from the original one.

1.3 Non-Accidentalness Principle

A parameterless algorithm needs to operate automatically and be based on criteria for making any decision required to provide the result. One of the main problems to be confronted in computer vision is how to decide if a structure is present or not, often related to the selection of detection thresholds. Unsurprisingly, the same issue arises in biological vision and perception; thus, the topic is discussed in computer vision literature and also in studies about perception. Many general principles have been proposed as rationale underlying perception [70]. Here we will concentrate on one of them, the *non-accidentalness* principle [3, 83].

As it is often the case, the non-accidentalness principle was independently introduced at least twice, by Witkin and Tenenbaum [87] and by I. Rock [72]; before that, it was implicitly used many times (e.g., [10, 56, 79, 82, 85]). Witkin and Tenenbaum introduced the idea while discussing the parallelism of curves and the rigidity of the motion of a set of dots:

> In its bare form, the argument says that what *looks* parallel or rigid really *is* parallel or rigid, less because parallelism is likely in any absolute sense, than because the spurious appearance of parallelism is extremely *un*likely to arise among causally unrelated curves. [87, p. 505, emphasis in the original]

In other words, an extremely particular viewpoint is required for nonparallel lines to become parallel. Rock describes the same idea with a temporal example and refers to it as *rejection-of-coincidence* or the *coincidence-explanation* principle:

> Certain well-known phenomena can be interpreted in terms of the rejection-of-coincidence principle. Consider the example of the launching effect described by Michotte: one visual object, A, moves until it reaches a second stationary object, B, whereupon A stops and B moves away in the appropriate direction and speed. The impression that A has caused B to move is irresistible. Not to perceive causation here is to accept the relationship between the behavior of the two objects as purely coincidental; the spatial and temporal contiguity, the shared direction of motion, and the equivalent velocity. [72, p. 137]

The principle is also related to previous ideas, as suggested by Rock:

> Therefore, if for "coincidence" one reads "improbable object or event" then does this principle not come down to Helmholtz' likelihood principle, namely, that we will tend to perceive those objects that would most likely be there to produce the given proximal stimulus? [72, p. 162]

This kind of argument, also present in [88], probably led Desolneux, Moisan, and Morel to call it the *Helmholtz principle* [19, 22]. Desolneux et al. stated the principle in two ways and each one of them adds new arguments to it. First, an empirical basis is given by "we do not perceive any structure in a uniform random image" [22, p. 31]. In this form it can be traced back to the work of Attneave [8] who observed that a random image produces the impression of homogeneity, which means that no structure is perceived. Attneave wanted to test empirically what was perceived when the retinal receptors were stimulated independently and thus generated what probably was the first synthetic random image. In this case, the non-accidentalness hypothesis is not applied to a configuration of the world but to the measurements on the sensors.

The second statement by Desolneux et al. is "whenever some large deviation from randomness occurs, a structure is perceived" [22, p. 31]. A new aspect is introduced here: structure is defined by its opposite. In the absence of structure, events are independent and behave randomly; structure contrasts by a more organized behavior. The strength of this argument is that it provides a limit to what should be considered structured by means of something usually easier to model: randomness.

Similar ideas underlie the use of classic statistical inference. The probability of a given observation is evaluated assuming the validity of a hypothesis being tested; the hypothesis is to be rejected when this probability is low, which would imply that the observation was accidental. In Fisher's words, "Either an exceptionally rare chance has occurred or the theory [hypothesis] is not true" [27, p. 39] (cited in [77]).

These concepts are linked to the usual sanity check performed by skeptics before accepting a hypothesis as valid: is the observation possible in the absence of the conjectured causal relation? For example, before accepting that telepathy is occurring one should check if communication is really taking place, i.e., is the error rate lower than what one would expect by chance? An example in astronomy was the discovery of several very precise alignment of quasars in the sky [7], later dismissed since these configurations could have arisen by chance [23, 80].

The non-accidentalness principle needs to be formalized to have a precise meaning. Strictly speaking, perfect coincidences are never observed because measurements are always carried out up to a certain precision. We need a way to evaluate non-accidentalness. As described by Lowe, "it is the degree to which some relation is unlikely to have arisen by accident which is the most important contributor to its significance" [55, p. 27]. For example, two straight lines may be observed to be parallel within 4 degrees; the chance that this relation would have arisen by chance is $4/180 = 1/45$. Similarly, Rock, discussing an example of illusory contours says "the more coincidence or otherwise unexplained regularity there is, the stronger the preference for the illusory-contour percept" [72, p. 141]. More precisely, Lowe proposed:

> As described above, we need to determine the probability that each relation in the image could have arisen by accident, $P(a)$. Naturally, the smaller that this value is, the more likely the relation is to have a causal interpretation. [55, p. 39]

In this proposal, the causal interpretation is accepted when that probability is small enough according to a threshold. Setting this threshold presents however some difficulties. As Lowe [55, p. 40] explains, the number of possible relations examined should be considered. If 10 line segments are observed, there are $10 \times (10 - 1)/2 = 45$ pairs to be tested for parallelism and one can expect to find a parallel pair within 4 degrees just by accident (because, as computed before, the chance of observing this precision is $1/45$ per pair). Still more parallel pairs are to be expected among 100 line segments and for the same accidental probability. A fixed probability threshold, thus, does not control the number of accidental observations and its value must be adapted to the size of the data.

Desolneux, Moisan, and Morel handled this problem in their *a contrario* approach. Instead of paying attention to the probability that an observation arises by accident, the focus is placed on the total number of accidental detections per image. The *a contrario* approach boils down to adjusting detection thresholds in order to bound by a fixed value the expected number of detections made in a random image of the same size as the one observed. The selected value indicates the average accidental (thus false) detections one is ready to accept per image. This methodology, based on the non-accidentalness principle, results in well-founded parameterless algorithms. A more detailed description of the *a contrario* approach will be made in the next chapter.

> *But is not an event in fact more significant and noteworthy the*
> *greater the number of fortuities necessary to bring it about?*
> Milan Kundera, "The Unbearable Lightness of Being"

1.4 Line Segment Detection

Line segments give important information about the geometric content of images. First, because most human-made objects contain intersecting flat surfaces; second, because many shapes accept an economic description in terms of straight lines. Line segments can be used as low-level features to extract information from images or can serve as a basic tool to analyze and detect more elaborated shapes.

Line segment detection is an old and recurrent problem in computer vision. Here we will mention just a few representative algorithms among the countless proposed in the last 40 years. Standard methods first apply the Canny edge detector [14] followed by a Hough transform [9, 40], extracting all lines that contain a number of edge points exceeding a threshold. These lines are thereafter cut into line segments by using gap and length thresholds. The Hough transform method has serious drawbacks. Textured regions that have a high edge density can cause many false detections (see the slanted lines on the tree of Fig. 1.3). Ignoring the orientation of the edge points, such algorithms obtain line segments with aberrant directions. Also, setting thresholds is a fundamental problem for any detection method. Using fixed thresholds can lead to a significant number of false positives or false negatives (see Fig. 1.3); these thresholds need to be adjusted for each image to produce useful results.

Another classic method starts from edge points, chains them into curves, and then cuts the chains into line segments by a straightness criterion [26]. A standard chaining method is due to Etemadi [25]. This method is parameterless and usually gives accurate results. Also, it is one of the few algorithms that simultaneously detect line segments and circular arcs.[2] Nevertheless, the result is not completely satisfactory, as illustrated in Fig. 1.3. Many detected straight and small edge curves are false positives: here comes the fundamental threshold problem again.

Burns, Hanson, and Riseman [13] introduced a linear-time line segment detection method with a key new idea. Their algorithm does not start with edge points, and actually ignores gradient magnitudes, using only gradient orientations. This algorithm was improved by Kahn, Kitchen, and Riseman [43, 44]. The line segments given by this algorithm are well localized, but the threshold problem is still there. The foliage of the tree in Fig. 1.3 could be described as a texture, as an object, but certainly not as a set of line segments. The examination of these methods suggests that a validation criterion should be added as a final step when aiming at parameterless algorithms.

There were some proposals of such criteria for the classic methods. A good example is the Progressive Probabilistic Hough Transform (PPHT) proposed by Matas, Galambos, and Kittler in [28, 60]. Like many similar methods, it accelerates the computing time by a random selection of the edge points. But the improvements came from the use of the image gradient information and a false detection control. Figure 1.3 shows a clear improvement over the standard Hough transform method. Nevertheless, the false detection control used is not completely satisfactory. First, the mechanism is well adapted for whole lines and not for line segment detection. Long line segments (similar in length to lines in the image) produce detections, but small ones do not. As a result, many short line segments are missing, as Fig. 1.3 shows. Second, the detection parameter of the method is, as proposed by

---

[2] The detected circular arcs are not shown in Fig. 1.3.

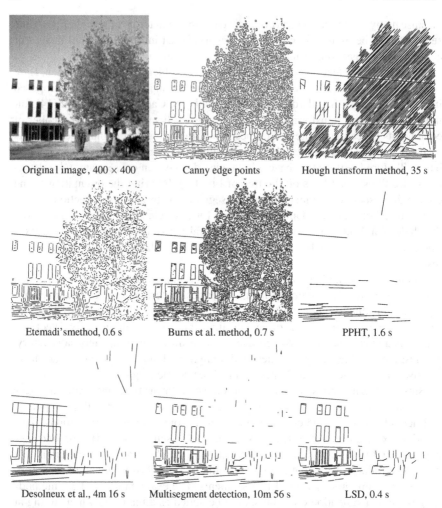

Fig. 1.3 A comparison of various line segment detection methods. The processing times on an Apple PowerBook G4 1.5 GHz are indicated. The Hough transform, Etemadi and Burns et al. methods detect many irrelevant small line segments on the tree. PPHT produces few false detections but fails to detect small line segments. Desolneux et al. controls the false detections but gives an inaccurate interpretation when aligned line segments are present. The multisegment detector gives a good result, but in prohibitive time. LSD gives a similar result in linear time

Lowe, the probability of getting a false detection each time an edge point is analyzed. But, the number of edge points analyzed depends on the image size and so does the expected number of false detections. The default value of this parameter is set to control false detections on image sizes of about 256×256. For larger images, the false detections are not controlled anymore, as the experiments in Figs. 4.17 and 4.18 will show. Any fixed value of this parameter will produce false detections on large enough images and will miss detections on small ones.

This threshold question was thoroughly analyzed by Desolneux, Moisan, and Morel [19, 22] using the *a contrario* approach and the non-accidentalness principle, described in the last section. Their line segment detection method succeeds in controlling the number of false positives with a parameterless algorithm. The method counts the number of aligned pixels (pixels with gradient direction approximately orthogonal to the line segment) and finds the line segments as outliers in a non-structured, *a contrario* model. Experimental evidence confirms that it indeed finds the line segments in the image where line segments are intuitively present. It has few false positives, as guaranteed by the method. Unfortunately, it often misinterprets arrays of aligned line segments (see, for example, the windows in Fig. 1.3). A detailed analysis of this defect was performed and a satisfactory solution is presented in [34, 37]. The solution involves a more sophisticated *a contrario* formulation, computing and comparing the meaningfulness of all possible arrays of line segments (multisegments) on each line. The misinterpretations of Desolneux et al.'s method were corrected, giving a much more accurate line segment detector (see Fig. 1.3). But Desolneux et al.'s and the multisegment detectors are exhaustive algorithms: Desolneux et al.'s method tests every possible line segment in the image and has an $O(N^4)$ complexity, where N is the image perimeter; the multisegment has an $O(N^5)$ complexity. Consequently, these detectors are doomed to be used only for offline applications.

The LSD algorithm [35, 36] provides a solution: instead of being exhaustive, a heuristic search is combined with the *a contrario* validation to produce a fast and parameterless algorithm. An improved version of Burns et al. method provides the heuristic that leads to a linear-time line segment detector (see Fig. 1.3). LSD will be described in full detail in Chap. 3, and its results analyzed in Chap. 4.

Chapter 2
A Contrario Detection

At the turn of the century, Desolneux, Moisan, and Morel undertook the task of formalizing the Gestalt theory into a mathematical framework [19, 22]. The motivation for this ambitious project was to provide a foundation for computer vision based, like the Gestalt theory [46, 51, 61, 62], on a small set of fundamental principles. They identified the lack of a principle to guide the selection of detection thresholds and their main contribution was to propose the *a contrario* framework to cover this need. This chapter will introduce the *a contrario* approach and its application to line segment detection.

The framework takes its name from the Latin expression "*a contrario*" which means *by or from contraries*. Accordingly, the meaning of a structure is derived from its *contrary*, the lack of structure: a stochastic model for unstructured data. The theory is actually a formalization of the non-accidentalness principle discussed in Sect. 1.3 (Desolneux et al. refer to it as *Helmholtz principle*). One would like to preclude detections on unstructured data. Yet, this is not possible: even if rarely, any structure *could* be observed in random data. The *a contrario* approach stipulates instead to set the detection thresholds in order to bound the *average* number of detections one would get on unstructured data. Figure 2.1 illustrates the idea.

We will start by an abstract presentation of these ideas, which should become more clear when illustrated in the next section by a simple example. Let us denote by H_0 the stochastic model for unstructured data. In our framework, the quality of a detection method will be evaluated relative to the *a contrario* model H_0. When the method is applied to unstructured data from H_0, every detection is a false detection. The mean number of detection events observed on data from H_0 corresponds then to the false detection rate of the method, and is the quantity to be bounded.

Any method will produce detections for certain configurations in the input data. We will call $\mathcal{E}$ the set of all possible detection events of a method: that is, all possible positions where the particular structure can be observed, together with the corresponding pixel configuration that makes it a valid detection. Every detection method defines, explicitly or implicitly, a set $\mathcal{E}$. The expected number of events from $\mathcal{E}$ in H_0 corresponds then to the expected number of false detections. Thus, a

R. Grompone von Gioi, *A Contrario Line Segment Detection*, SpringerBriefs in Computer Science, DOI 10.1007/978-1-4939-0575-1_2, © The Author(s) 2014

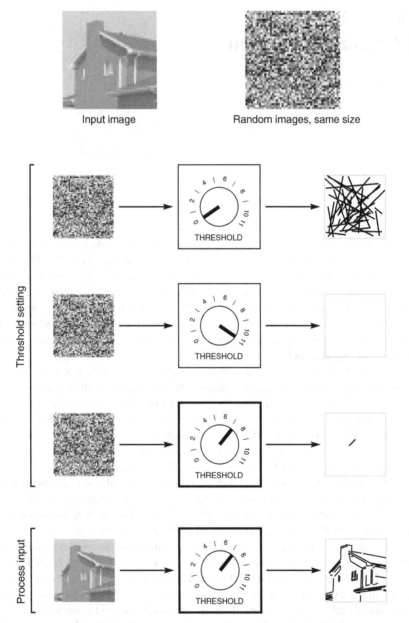

Fig. 2.1 An intuitive illustration of the *a contrario* approach. Different threshold values are tried in random data of the same size as the input. A low detection threshold produces a large number of detections in random data, all of them accidental (*first row*). A high threshold rejects accidental detections, but never produces detections at all (*second row*). The *a contrario* approach suggests selecting thresholds that produce, on average, a fixed number of detections in random data (one in this case, third row). This is restrictive enough to reject most detections by chance, allowing as many good detections as possible. Once the threshold is selected with random data, the algorithm is applied to the input. For simple problems as line segment detection, it is possible to compute the right thresholds analytically, without the need to simulate random data

detection method is said to define ε-meaningful events (or to produce ε-meaningful detections), when the expected number of false detections is bounded by ε.

The *a contrario* statistical framework rests on the definition of ε-meaningful events, relative to a stochastic model H_0 for unstructured data:

Definition 1. The events of a set $\mathscr{E}$ are called ε-meaningful events in H_0 if the *expected* total number of these events observed under H_0 is less than or equal to ε.

As we will see, setting the constant ε to a small fixed value results in an effective control of the number of false detections.

The *a contrario* framework is closely related to the theory of statistical analysis. The problem is formulated as a set of statistical tests in the spirit of Fisherian statistics [16, 41], but including corrections for *multiple comparisons* [38, 39]; see [22, section 15.3.2] and [67, section 4.4] for a comparison. A similar framework was proposed by Dembski [18] for a different problem: the detection of "intelligent causes" relative to "natural causes". This chapter is a brief introduction to the *a contrario* approach; for more details refer to [22].

2.1 A Simple Example

Let us consider a sequence of coin flips: a random sequence of equally likely heads and tails. It is not surprising to observe a sequence of three consecutive heads. Actually, this event should appear once every eight sets of three coin tosses. Now, imagine that a sequence of 100 heads is observed. That would be an extremely unlikely event with a fair coin. Even if everyone in the world made a flip per second, it would take about 1,000 billion years before someone could get that result just by chance. Observing such a sequence would be an overwhelmingly lucky event, and it is more reasonable to look for a causal connection of some kind. However, following the non-accidentalness principle, *only* events that cannot be explained by chance require a causal explanation.

There is another important point to reflect on. Let 1 be heads and 0 tails. Then, the following sequence represents a possible result of 50 coin tosses:

11111111111111111111111111111111111111111111111111.

Such a sequence of 50 consecutive heads is very structured and unexpected. The probability of observing this sequence with a fair coin is 2^{-50}. In contrast, the following one seems unstructured:

01010010001000011000001100110001100111010011001000.

Actually, the probability of observing *exactly* the latter sequence is the same as before, 2^{-50}, as it is given by the product of the probabilities for each individual equi-probable event: getting a tail in the first toss (1/2), getting a head on the second toss (1/2), a tail in the third one (1/2), and so on. Both sequences are hence equally likely (or unlikely). What makes the former a relevant event cannot be *only* its small probability. While the first sequence has a certain regularity, a certain order that makes it particular, the second one has no particular reason to be differentiated from, for example,

00110011100110110100100100010100011010100000111100.

Dembski [18], discussing the problem of the identification of intelligent causes, states that a relevant event must have a small probability and also be *specified*, meaning that it should conform to a previously defined pattern. To illustrate the point, Dembski suggests imagining an archer shooting arrows at a target painted on the wall; the arrow hitting the center of the target would be a relevant event. However, if the target is painted on the wall around the arrow *after* shooting, the event would not be relevant at all. Analogously, a relevant pattern must be defined in advance— for example, a sequence of n heads—and not be selected as any particular observed pattern that happens with low probability.

Getting back to the *a contrario* approach, two parts need to be defined: an observing method to measure the structure, and a model for unstructured data. The former specifies the structure (the pattern) in advance; in the previous analogy, it corresponds to drawing the target for the archer. The latter tells us what to expect in a random case; think of a blind archer. The *a contrario* approach advises to apply thresholds on the observations and to choose its values to allow, on average, only ε detections on unstructured data. This results in ε-meaningful detections in agreement with definition 1. The smaller the value of ε, the less number of false detections accepted, and the more strict the conditions imposed on the structure to be detected. To continue with the previous analogy, the smaller the ε, the smaller the target where the archer is aiming and the more meaningful if the arrow hits it.

Consider a simple toy detection problem: we want to detect when someone is pressing a certain button. Imagine there is a mechanism that measures the state of the button, giving the value 1 when pressed and 0 when released. In an ideal case, an observed sequence would be as follows,

00000000000111111111111111110000000000000000000000,

indicating that the button was first released, then pressed, and finally released again. Unfortunately, our systems is corrupted by noise and a typical observation looks more like:

01001001000111111111111111110010000101100110001100.

To simplify things, let us assume that noise only affects released buttons, but a pressed button always produces the value 1. Judging the button as pressed whenever a 1 is observed would lead to many false detections. However, a long enough run of 1s would certainly correspond to a pressed button. How much is *long enough*? The *a contrario* approach proposes to define the threshold in order to control the number of false detections due to noise.

Let us formalize the problem. We observe some data x, a binary sequence in our example, and we want to detect a given structure: an exceptional long run of consecutive 1s. The structure can be located at various positions and each one is a candidate that must be tested; a family of N_C candidates $\mathscr{C} = \{c_1, \ldots, c_{N_C}\}$ is defined. We will call N_C the number of tests. In our case, runs of 1s can start at any element of the binary sequence; thus, N_C is equal to the length L of the binary sequence x. (We ignore the fact that the run in the last position has a length of at most one element.) We can now define the observing method: a function $k(c_i, x)$ to measure the degree to which the sought structure is present in data x at candidate position c_i. For our problem, the value $k(c_i, x)$ is the length of the run of consecutive 1s starting at position c_i.

The second part to be defined is a stochastic model H_0 for unstructured binary sequences. The simplest choice for the present example is the classic model of fair coin tosses: independent flips with equal probability for heads and tails.

To complete the detection procedure we need to specify thresholds κ_i so that a candidate c_i is validated as a detection in data x when $k(c_i, x) \geq \kappa_i$. Given an observation x, the total number of detections is then

$$d(x) = \sum_{i=1}^{N_C} \mathbb{1}_{k(c_i, x) \geq \kappa_i},$$

where $\mathbb{1}_A$ is the indicator function, taking the value 1 in the set (or event) A and zero otherwise. The *a contrario* approach requires that the thresholds κ_i be set so that the expected number of detections $d(X)$, when X is random data from the model H_0, be less than or equal to ε. Since there are many κ_i and a single ε, there are many ways to achieve this adjustment. A common one is the so-called "Bonferroni correction" [39]. It consists in dividing up ε in equal parts among the tests, which amounts to authorize the same number of false detections per candidate. This comes to setting

$$\kappa_i = \min\left\{n, \mathbb{P}[k(c_i, X) \geq n] \leq \frac{\varepsilon}{N_C}\right\}. \tag{2.1}$$

With the thresholds κ_i defined this way, we can show that the expected number of detections in H_0 is controlled by ε and thus the detections are ε-meaningful events:

Proposition 1. *The family $\mathscr{E}$ of N_C events $\{k(c_i, X) \geq \kappa_i\}$, with κ_i defined as in (2.1), are ε-meaningful events when X is data from H_0.*

Proof. The expected number of events observed is

$$\mathbb{E}[d(X)] = \mathbb{E}\left[\sum_{i=1}^{N_C} \mathbb{1}_{k(c_i, X) \geq \kappa_i}\right] = \sum_{i=1}^{N_C} \mathbb{P}[k(c_i, X) \geq \kappa_i],$$

where $\mathbb{E}$ is the expectation operator and X is random data drawn from H_0. But by definition of κ_i we know that

$$\mathbb{P}[k(c_i, X) \geq \kappa_i] \leq \frac{\varepsilon}{N_C}.$$

Then,

$$\mathbb{E}[d(X)] \le \sum_{i=1}^{N_C} \frac{\varepsilon}{N_C} = \varepsilon \, ,$$

which concludes the proof.   □

In the *a contrario* framework a specific quantity, $\mathrm{NFA}(c_i, x)$, is associated to the candidate c_i observed in data x. It is defined as the number of tests considered, times the probability of observing events at least as meaningful in the *a contrario* model H_0:

$$\mathrm{NFA}(c_i, x) = N_C \cdot \mathbb{P}[k(c_i, X) \ge k(c_i, x)] \, . \tag{2.2}$$

Note that the larger the observed measure $k(c_i, x)$, the lower the probability that $k(c_i, X) \ge k(c_i, x)$ in H_0; therefore, the smaller the NFA value, and the more meaningful the observation is. This quantity was devised to provide a handy test to validate events: an observation (c_i, x) is ε-meaningful if and only if $\mathrm{NFA}(c_i, x) \le \varepsilon$. It is easy to check that this is the case since this test is equivalent to

$$\mathbb{P}[k(c_i, X) \ge k(c_i, x)] \le \frac{\varepsilon}{N_C} \, ,$$

which implies, in turn, that $k(c_i, x) \ge \kappa_i$, as is required for ε-meaningfulness.

The name NFA stands for *Number of False Alarms* and is justified by the following fact: a candidate c_i in data x with $\mathrm{NFA}(c_i, x) = \alpha$ will be validated as a detection only if ε is larger than or equal to α, and in such case the method will get at least α false detections. In other words, $\mathrm{NFA}(c_i, x)$ corresponds to the false detection level needed to accept the event.

The constant ε corresponds to the expected number of false detections that one is ready to accept, which depends on the task being handled. If we are trying to detect an event that is rarely observed, accepting one false detection on average would make the detector useless: In such a case, the expected number of detections would be, numerically, very similar to the probability of a false detection, and the *a contrario* framework would be less useful. This framework is well adapted for the case when many detections are made in a typical case and thus accepting a few false detections is not a problem. In pictures of artificial environments, for example, one would expect many line segment detections, as it is shown in Fig. 1.1; to get *one* false detection among them is not a real problem. It is important, however, that the detector keeps the number of false detections controlled to a fixed value ε for different data sets, preventing the explosion of false detections when the data size grows. What value should be used for ε? The thresholds κ_i show a slow dependency on ε, which implies that the resulting method is not very dependent on the particular ε value selected. Any small value is usually fine. As a simple convention, Desolneux et al. [19, 22] suggest using $\varepsilon = 1$. We will see some examples in the next section.

Let us complete the formulation for our example. We need to compute the probability $\mathbb{P}[k(c_i, X) \ge n]$ of observing a run of at least n consecutive 1s starting at position c_i. Given the independence of the digits in binary sequences under H_0, that quantity is equal to the probability that the first n digits, starting at c_i, are all 1. (The following digits could include more consecutive 1s, increasing the length of the run, or not.) We have

$$\mathbb{P}[k(c_i, X) \geq n] = p^n \, ,$$

where p is the probability of getting a 1 under H_0. As computed before, the number of tests N_C is the length L of the binary sequence. Then, the NFA value of an observed run of length $k(c_i, x)$ is given by

$$\mathrm{NFA}(c_i, x) = L\, p^{k(c_i, x)} \, .$$

For sequences of total length 50, as the previous ones, and with $p = 1/2$, the NFA value of a run of length n is given by 50×2^{-n}. Table 2.1 shows some numerical values. As one could anticipate, we will observe on average 25 runs of at least one element, which is not a meaningful event. A similar conclusion is made for runs of two, three, or four elements. Runs of at least six consecutive 1s are more meaningful, as it is not expected to be present in every data set from H_0. The meaningfulness grows with the length of the run. With $\varepsilon = 1$, runs of length six or more are considered detections. This threshold will produce no detection in a typical random binary sequence of length 50,

11101111101000111001000110100101111011010100001000,

whereas when meaningful events are present, they will be detected,

00101111111111111101000010011010011111111100100011.

Setting $\varepsilon = 1$ implies getting, on average, one false detection per sequence; that is, one detection per random binary sequence from H_0. It may seem futile to accept one false detection for such a short sequence, but the strength of the method lies in how it adapts the thresholds automatically to larger data sets. If we now observe a sequence of one million digits, $L = 10^6$, the limit case for $\varepsilon = 1$ is runs of 20 heads with an NFA value of 0.95. We will get all the meaningful runs and still get at most *one* false detection in sequences of one million digits. The limit run length is given by

$$n_{\mathrm{th}} = \left\lceil \frac{\log \varepsilon - \log N_C}{\log p} \right\rceil ,$$

where $\lceil x \rceil$ is the smallest integer not less than x. The dependencies on ε and on the number of tests N_C are opposite and both logarithmic, which implies a slight dependency. This is usually the case for *a contrario* formulations.

Table 2.1 NFA values for runs of n consecutive 1s on a binary sequence of total length 50

n	NFA	n	NFA	n	NFA	n	NFA
1	25	6	0.78	11	$2 \cdot 10^{-2}$	16	$8 \cdot 10^{-4}$
2	12.5	7	0.39	12	$1 \cdot 10^{-2}$	17	$4 \cdot 10^{-4}$
3	6.25	8	0.195	13	$6 \cdot 10^{-3}$	18	$2 \cdot 10^{-4}$
4	3.13	9	0.098	14	$3 \cdot 10^{-3}$	19	$9 \cdot 10^{-5}$
5	1.56	10	0.049	15	$1 \cdot 10^{-3}$	20	$5 \cdot 10^{-5}$

2.2 *A Contrario* Line Segment Detection

Let us see now how these ideas apply to a detection problem in computer vision. We will follow Desolneux, Moisan, and Morel [19] and introduce their line segment detector. We are looking for locally straight edges in images. This can be done by testing all possible line segments and for each one checking if there is an edge that roughly follows it. We will use the simplest of image indicators that provides information about edges: the image gradient.

A digital image x is defined as a grid of $N \times M$ pixels, each one with a numerical value representing its brightness: small values correspond to dark pixels and large values to bright ones. In a common representation, pixels take values in the range $[0, 255]$, zero corresponding to black and 255 to white. The gradient of an image at a certain pixel is a vector pointing in the direction of maximum increase of image brightness, see Fig. 2.2. The gradient is actually locally orthogonal to the image level-lines; that is, lines where the image brightness is constant. When an edge is present at a given pixel, the level-line angle roughly follows the edge and the gradient vector is roughly orthogonal to the edge, see Fig. 2.2. Computing the local level-line angle at each pixel results in a *level-line field*, see Fig. 2.3, whose elements are well structured along edges. Notice that the level-line elements are oriented, implicitly indicating which side of the level-line is darker. In what follows, $\lambda(u, v)$ will denote the (oriented) level-line angle at coordinates (u, v). The gradient magnitude gives additional information about the strength of the edge, but this information will not be used here. The precise definition of the image gradient to be used will be described in Sect. 2.3.

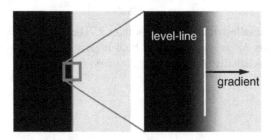

Fig. 2.2 An edge, the image gradient, and a level-line

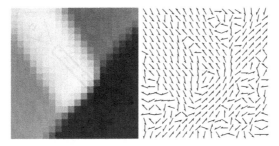

Fig. 2.3 An image (*left*) and its level-line field (*right*). Notice that the level-line elements are oriented, implicitly indicating which side of the level-line is darker

The proposal of Desolneux et al. [19, 22] for detecting line segments is simple: for each candidate, count the number of pixels along it where the level-line angle is compatible with the line segment. *Compatible* means that they have the same direction up to a tolerance τ, see Fig. 2.4. These pixels define the τ-*aligned pixels*, or *aligned* pixels for short:

Definition 2 (τ-aligned pixel). A pixel at coordinates (u,v) is called a τ-*aligned pixel* with a line segment s when the level-line angle at that pixel, $\lambda(u,v)$, shares the same orientation as the line segment up to a precision τ:

$$\left|\text{Angle}\big(\lambda(u,v),s\big)\right| \leq \tau.$$

Depending on the number of *aligned* pixels, it will be decided whether a line segment is present or not.

Here is where the *a contrario* approach and the non-accidentalness principle come into play. A candidate will be validated only when its observation corresponds to an unlikely event in the absence of a causal interpretation, that is, in an unstructured image. As in the example of the last section, we need to define a family $\mathscr{S}$ of N_{tests} candidates s_i to test, an observed variable $k(s_i,x)$, and an *a contrario* model H_0. With these elements we will define the NFA of an observation and the constant ε will complete the method.

The family $\mathscr{S}$ includes all the line segments whose end points are centered in pixels of the image. In an $N \times M$ image we have NM possible initial points and NM possible end points; thus $N_{\text{tests}} = (NM)^2$. Notice that the line segments are *oriented*, meaning that the order of their starting and ending points is not arbitrary: an edge is a transition from dark to bright, and the orientation of a line segment indicates which is the dark side. The resolution of digital images is limited by its discrete nature; for that reason, this family of $(NM)^2$ candidates is rich enough to contain all the relevant line segments.[1]

---

[1] The family $\mathscr{S}$ does not include all the possible line segments in the image; it does not include all the *discrete* line segments, either. There is an extensive literature on the subject of *digital straightness* [47, 73]. Consider an $N \times N$ grid of pixel centers. A *digital straight line* is a set of points in the grid that corresponds to the digitalization of a line. For example, the line $y = ax + b$, has a

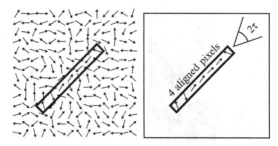

Fig. 2.4 *Left*: a line segment candidate shown over the level-line field. *Right*: the number of aligned pixels, up to an angular tolerance of τ, is counted. The candidate shown has four aligned pixels among seven

As stated before, the observed variable $k(s,x)$ for candidate s in image x is the number of *aligned* pixels in the line segment. For this count, the line segment is defined as a rectangle of width equal to one pixel, see Fig. 2.4. Given a candidate line segment s, we will denote by $n(s)$ the total number of pixels in the corresponding rectangle. The validation then takes into account that $k(s,x)$ aligned pixels were observed among a total of $n(s)$ pixels.

The only information measured from the image are the level-line angles. Hence, Desolneux et al. [22] proposed a stochastic model H_0 for unstructured level-line fields satisfying the following properties:

- $\{\lambda(u,v)\}$ is a family of independent random variables,
- $\lambda(u,v)$ is uniformly distributed over $[0,2\pi]$,

where $\lambda(u,v)$ is the level-line angle at pixel (u,v). Notice that this is a stochastic model for a *level-line field* and not for an image. Strictly speaking, the data x should be defined as this field; to simplify notation and because no real risk of confusion is present, we will use x when referring to an image or to its level-line field.

This model corresponds indeed to unstructured level-line fields: there is no relation between the values at different pixels and the values show an isotropic distribution. The choice can also be justified in the fact that, under certain sampling conditions, this model corresponds to the level-line field of white noise images, see [22, p. 67]. As shown by Attneave [8], white noise images produce an impression of homogeneity, which corresponds to no detection in human vision. Moreover, this model represents well isotropic zones, while straight edges are exactly the opposite: highly anisotropic zones. Thus, in practice a set of pixels will not be accepted as a line segment if it could have been formed by an isotropic process. A good example is shown in Fig. 1.3. The foliage of the tree is far from being a white noise process, but it is an isotropic structure; as a consequence, no line segment will be validated by the *a contrario* approach.

---

corresponding digital line $\{(n,y_n) : n = 1,2,\ldots,N, \ y_n = \lfloor an+b \rfloor, \ 1 \leq y_n \leq N\}$. Just the digital straight *lines* on an $N \times N$ grid are $O(N^4)$, see [52]. Moreover, in most cases there are multiple digital straight line *segments* defined by the same end points; for example, $\{(1,1),(1,2),(1,3),(2,4)\}$ and $\{(1,1),(2,2),(2,3),(2,4)\}$ are both digital straight line segments from $(1,1)$ to $(2,4)$.

We are now in a position to define the NFA for a candidate line segment s in an image x using the general formulation of the previous section:

$$\text{NFA}(s,x) = N_{\text{tests}} \cdot \mathbb{P}[k(s,X) \geq k(s,x)] \,,$$

where X is a level-line field according to the model H_0.

Given the isotropic angle distribution under H_0, the probability that any individual pixel is τ-*aligned* with a line segment s is $p = \frac{\tau}{\pi}$. The number of aligned pixels in the *a contrario* model, $k(s,X)$, can be expressed as the sum $A_1 + A_2 + \cdots + A_{n(s)}$, where A_j are Bernoulli variables taking the value 1 if the pixel j is aligned to the line segment s or zero otherwise. Due to the independence at different pixels in H_0, the variables A_j are independent and identically distributed; thus, its sum $k(s,X)$ follows a binomial distribution and,

$$\mathbb{P}[k(s,X) \geq k(s,x)] = B\big(n(s), k(s,x), p\big) \,,$$

where $B(n,k,p)$ is the tail of the binomial distribution:

$$B(n,k,p) = \sum_{t=k}^{n} \binom{n}{t} p^t (1-p)^{n-t} \,.$$

Putting all together we get the NFA value associated to an observation:

$$\text{NFA}(s,x) = (NM)^2 \cdot B\big(n(s), k(s,x), p\big) \,. \tag{2.3}$$

As in the last section, the NFA value corresponds to the expected number of line segments in H_0 which are as good as s. A large NFA value means that similar events appear often by chance and the structure is not relevant; inversely, a small NFA value reflects an unlikely and meaningful event. Line segment candidates with $\text{NFA}(s,x) \leq \varepsilon$ are kept as detections and are called ε-*meaningful line segments*. The formulation is exactly the same as in the previous section and, as before, we can show that the method satisfies the non-accidentalness principle to a level ε:

Proposition 2. *Line segments with* $\text{NFA} \leq \varepsilon$ *are* ε-*meaningful events. Equivalently,*

$$\mathbb{E}\left[\sum_{s \in \mathscr{S}} \mathbb{1}_{\text{NFA}(s,X) \leq \varepsilon}\right] \leq \varepsilon$$

where $\mathbb{E}$ *is the expectation operator,* $\mathbb{1}$ *is the indicator function,* $\mathscr{S}$ *is the family of line segments considered, and* X *is a random image on* H_0.

Proof. We define $\hat{k}(s)$ as

$$\hat{k}(s) = \min\left\{\kappa \in \mathbb{N}, \ \mathbb{P}[k(s,X) \geq \kappa] \leq \frac{\varepsilon}{N_{\text{tests}}}\right\} \,.$$

Then, $\text{NFA}(s,x) \le \varepsilon$ is equivalent to $k(s,x) \ge \hat{k}(s)$. Now,

$$\mathbb{E}\left[\sum_{s \in \mathscr{S}} \mathbb{1}_{\text{NFA}(s,X) \le \varepsilon}\right] = \sum_{s \in \mathscr{S}} \mathbb{P}\left[\text{NFA}(s,X) \le \varepsilon\right] = \sum_{s \in \mathscr{S}} \mathbb{P}\left[k(s,X) \ge \hat{k}(s)\right] .$$

But, by definition of $\hat{k}(s)$ we know that

$$\mathbb{P}\left[k(s,X) \ge \hat{k}(s)\right] \le \frac{\varepsilon}{N_{\text{tests}}} ,$$

and using that $\#\mathscr{S} = N_{\text{tests}}$ we get

$$\mathbb{E}\left[\sum_{s \in \mathscr{S}} \mathbb{1}_{\text{NFA}(s,X) \le \varepsilon}\right] \le \sum_{s \in \mathscr{S}} \frac{\varepsilon}{N_{\text{tests}}} = \varepsilon ,$$

which concludes the proof. $\square$

Proposition 2 guarantees that false detections are controlled in H_0. For the same reasons as before, we set $\varepsilon = 1$, once and for all.

Figure 2.5 shows an example of applying the described method on a simple noisy image. The validation step did a good job: detections are made *only* where edges are present in the image. However, the detection result is not completely satisfactory. Each straight edge in the image produces many redundant line segment detections, differing in the exact localization, angle and length. Also, many of them are markedly longer than the corresponding edges: any line segment with a significant overlap with an image edge will produce a detection. In addition, the exhaustive test of $(NM)^2$ line segments requires considerable computing time.

The next three sections will discuss in detail several aspects of this basic algorithm. Then, Sect. 2.6 will discuss further improvements to the basic algorithm to cope with the redundancy disadvantages just mentioned.

2.3 Gradient Computation and Sampling

The theory of *a contrario* line segment detection presented in this chapter entails a control of the number of false detections in white noise. As shown, the number of false detections can be bounded assuming independent pixel gradient orientations (orthogonal to level-line orientations). This independence relies on a trade-off between the support of the discrete operator chosen to approximate the gradient and the discretization resolution. If the gradient is computed using a 2×2 support,

$$\nabla x(u,v) = \begin{pmatrix} \frac{x(u+1,v)+x(u+1,v+1)-x(u,v)-x(u,v+1)}{2} \\ \frac{x(u,v+1)+x(u+1,v+1)-x(u,v)-x(u+1,v)}{2} \end{pmatrix} , \tag{2.4}$$

the algorithm should only consider pixels at a distance larger than two, in order to guarantee the potential independence of their gradient orientation.

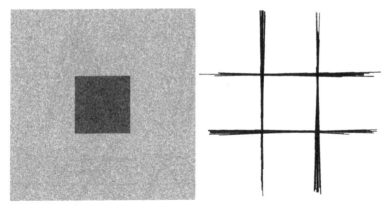

Fig. 2.5 An example of line segment detection by Desolneux, Moisan, and Morel's method [19]

One way to do this is to drop one pixel out of two along the end points of the line segment. But with the pixels, some information is dropped too. If all pixels are kept, the unstructured model H_0 of Sect. 2.2 is not valid as adjacent pixels necessarily have dependent gradient angles. It is still possible to build an *a contrario* method, but a theoretical bound for the number of false detections under the dependency model is much harder to get. However, numerical experiments on white noise show that the number of false detections does not blow up when all pixels in the discretization are kept, and we assume independence. This is an empirical verification that the non-accidentalness principle is still valid without any down-sampling. The advantage of using all pixels instead of one out of two is the ability to detect finer structures; Fig. 2.6 shows two examples.

To test experimentally the number of false detections, two sets of $N \times N$ level-line fields were generated [34]. In the first one, the theoretical conditions of H_0 are satisfied; that is, all level-line angles are independent and isotropic. The second set was generated by directly computing the level-line field on $N \times N$ white noise images using the operator in (2.4); the angles obtained are uniformly distributed in $[0, 2\pi]$ as shown in [22, p. 67], but adjacent angles are dependent. Let us call these sets "independent gradient" and "dependent gradient", respectively. Desolneux et al.'s algorithm as described in Sect. 2.2 was applied to each of the level-line fields in each of the two sets, and for various values of ε. Table 2.2 shows the mean number of detections for each of the two sets. We want to compare the number of false detections; we set ε to large values to see the effect more clearly.

Note that in the "independent gradient" set that corresponds to the theoretical *a contrario* model, the mean number of false detections is smaller than ε, about the half. This offset is due to the discrete nature of the binomial distribution: The number of *aligned* pixels k in a line segment is an integer quantity; thus, the detection threshold κ will be set to the largest *integer* for which

$$\text{NFA} = (NM)^2 \cdot B(n, \kappa, p) \leq \varepsilon .$$

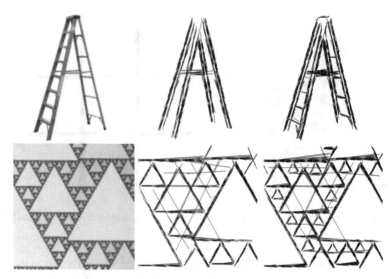

Fig. 2.6 Two examples of the improved resolution obtained by using all pixels instead of one out of two. *Left:* input images, 144×151 and 130×130 pixels. *Center:* meaningful line segments using one-out-of-two pixels. *Right:* meaningful line segments using all pixels. The steps of the ladder are only detected when all pixels are used. In the second case, smaller triangles are detected when using all pixels. No false detection occurs

In a typical case, the NFA value obtained for κ will not be exactly ε, but considerably smaller. This effect, acting on the whole family of tests, leads to offset observed in Table 2.2, see [33] for more details.

The number of false detections observed in Table 2.2 has the same order of magnitude for the independent and dependent cases. The numbers obtained are very similar, suggesting that the same detection thresholds can be used for the dependent case without a degradation of the number of false detections. In fact it can be checked that gradient orientations at neighboring pixels computed with a 2×2 mask are fairly decorrelated in white noise (the correlation between neighbor angles is about 0.2). Moreover, a study performed by Pătrăucean [67] using Markov process models suggests that this dependency may actually *decrease* the number of false detections. In such a case, the *a contrario* framework is still satisfied and the control of false detections is still achieved.

To sum up, we do not know the exact detection thresholds to take into consideration the dependency induced by the gradient computation mask, but the empirical evidence is strong enough to support the use of the same thresholds as for the independent case.

Table 2.2 A measure of the sensitivity of Desolneux, Moisan, and Morel's algorithm to the dependency of pixels. The table shows the mean number of detections in 100 white noise images of size 50×50 for different values of ε. The offset between the mean number of detections in H_0 and ε observed in both cases is due to the discrete nature of the binomial distribution, see [33] for details

ε	100,000	10,000	1,000	100	10	1
Independent gradient	50,590	4,291	395.9	40.06	3.96	0.41
Dependent gradient	50,976	4,300	388.2	37.51	3.61	0.25

2.4 Angular Precision

Desolneux et al.'s algorithm depends on the choice for the angular precision p, related to the angular tolerance τ by $p = \frac{\tau}{\pi}$. The *a contrario* approach will control the number of false detections independently of the precision p used, but the usefulness of the method as an line segment detector can vary with its value. Extreme values would render the method useless: a value $p = 1$ would never produce detections and with $p = 0$ only perfect straight edges would be detected, rendering the method too sensitive to noise.

What value should be used? Considering that our aim is to detect straight edges, a reasonable requirement is $p \leq 1/4$, which corresponds to angles of ± 45 degrees relative to the perfect orientation. For angles larger than 45 degrees, the meaning of being *aligned* to the edge dissolves and *orthogonal* to the edge becomes a better description. Due to image noise induced by acquisition and quantization, and due to imperfection of edges, it is rare to observe precision finer than $p = 1/64$. In practice, the range of $1/4$ to $1/32$ is good enough: coarser precision improves little the robustness to noise and finer precision seldom occurs [22, p. 66].

The selection of p also implies a compromise between robustness to noise and the ability to detect short line segments. Consider that the level-line elements shown in Fig. 2.7 are observed in a 100×100 image. With a precision $p = 1/32$ we get six aligned pixels for A, but *zero* aligned pixels in the noisier case B; the latter will not produce a detection while the former, with $\mathrm{NFA}_A^{p=1/32} = 100^4 \cdot 32^{-6} \approx 0.09$, will be considered 1-meaningful. Inversely, with $p = 1/8$ we get six aligned pixels in A and nine aligned pixels in B. Now, $\mathrm{NFA}_A^{p=1/8} = 100^4 \cdot 8^{-6} \approx 381.5$ and $\mathrm{NFA}_B^{p=1/8} = 100^4 \cdot 8^{-9} \approx 0.75$ so B is 1-meaningful, but A is not.

No fixed precision will get all detections at the same time: fine precisions are able to detect short line segments but are sensitive to noise, large precisions are robust to noise, but cannot detect short line segments. Values like $p = 1/16$ or $1/8$ are usually the best choices.

Even better is to use a multi-precision p approach: apply the same method repeatedly, but for different values of p, for example $1/64, 1/32, 1/16, 1/8,$ and $1/4$. In such a case, we need to make some adjustments so that the resulting method still controls the number of false detections. Indeed, if we apply γ times the original method but with different values of p, we would get ε false detections for each one,

Fig. 2.7 Two sets of level-line elements. *A*: six pixels with precision $1/32$, (± 5.6 degrees). *B*: nine pixels with precision $1/8$, (± 22.5 degrees)

a total of $\gamma \varepsilon$ false detections and γ times more than desired. There are different ways to correct the method to obtain again an average of ε false detections. One is to count in N_{tests} all the tests for different precisions. But the simpler one is to *divide* ε among the γ different detectors applied. Each detector would have an allowance of ε/γ false detections; summing all together, the multi-p method will produce, on average, ε false detections.

2.5 Continuous Angular Measurement

The last section made clear the need to use different values for the precision p to have a good compromise between accuracy and robustness to noise. It is natural to attempt to handle all precisions at the same time, using continuous statistics instead of the binomial ones [33].

In the original Desolneux et al.'s method, an observation consists of a binary sequence $(a_1, \ldots, a_n)$, where a_j take the values zero or one according to whether the j-th pixel is τ-aligned or not. In other words, the angle information is quantized with precision τ. Alternatively, we can keep the level-line angle information as is. Let us normalize the angles between 0 and 1, zero meaning a perfect alignment and one meaning the level-line is opposed to the line segment. Now a_j take values in the full interval $[0, 1]$.

The space of possible configurations $(a_1, \ldots, a_n)$ defines a unit hypercube of n dimensions with one vertex at the origin, see Fig. 2.8. The perfect line segment corresponds to the configuration $(0, 0, \ldots, 0)$ and the worst one to $(1, 1, \ldots, 1)$. But now, instead of restricting ourselves to the vertices of the hypercube, as in Desolneux et al.'s detector, any point of it is a valid configuration. Given a candidate c in an image x, a configuration $(a_1, \ldots, a_n)$ is determined, and the measure $k(c, x)$ that evaluates the quality of line segments is a real-valued function defined on the hypercube. This function defines a family of iso-$k(c, x)$ surfaces inside the hypercube that we will call *frontiers*. For example, a value α gives the frontier surface $k(c, x) = \alpha$.

Given the function $k(c, x)$, the *a contrario* approach does the rest. The unstructured model H_0 defined in Sect. 2.2, with independent and uniformly distributed level-line angles, induces a uniform distribution on the hypercube of configurations. The probability of an observed event, $\mathbb{P}[k(c, X) \geq k(c, x)]$, is then obtained by integrating the uniform distribution under the frontier surface defined by the value of $k(c, x)$.

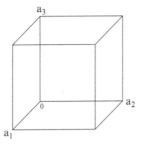

Fig. 2.8 Hypercube of possible configurations, shown for $n = 3$

The selection of the function k, or equivalently of the frontier family, needs some discussion. A simple idea is to use functions of the form $k(c,x) = \sum_j f(a_j)$, where a_j is the normalized angle at pixel j in the candidate and f is some function on the normalized angles. A natural choice for f is $f_A(a) = -a$, that defines an *additive* family of frontiers of the form $a_1 + a_2 + \cdots + a_n = \alpha$, see Fig. 2.9 left. Notice the minus sign to obtain the largest value for the perfect alignment. A second option is the *multiplicative* frontiers family $a_1 \cdot a_2 \cdots a_n = \alpha$, see Fig. 2.9 right. This corresponds to using $f_M(a) = -\log(a)$. These two frontier families were proposed in [33] and a similar formulation but with a different class of f functions was proposed before in [42].

The multiplicative family presents a small drawback: The presence of *one* perfectly aligned pixel, $a_j = 0$, is enough to produce a meaningful line segment, regardless of the angle direction of the other pixels. Nevertheless, this problem is not new. In the binomial formulation, if the value of p is chosen small enough, one aligned pixel will also lead to a meaningful line segment. On the other hand, $a_j = 0$ should never happen, except in synthetic images. Unfortunately, due to the discretization of pixel values this can happen in practice. The problem has a simple (although not elegant) solution by imposing a minimum attainable precision in the measurement, so a_j can never be zero.

We need to compute

$$\text{NFA}(c,x) = N_{\text{tests}} \cdot \mathbb{P}[k(c,X) \geq k(c,x)] \;.$$

The probability term is determined by the volume of the hypercube under the frontier defined by $k(c,x)$.

For the additive case, the frontier is the hyperplane $a_1 + \cdots + a_n = -k_A(c,x)$ and the sought probability is determined by the intersection of the unit hypercube with the half-plane $a_1 + \cdots + a_n \leq -k_A(c,x)$. This computation is straightforward when $\alpha = a_1 + \cdots + a_n \leq 1$ because the intersection is the standard simplex of size α. The volume of this simplex is $\frac{\alpha^n}{n!}$, see [78]. Then,

$$\mathbb{P}[k_A(c,X) \geq k_A(c,x)] = \frac{[-k_A(c,x)]^n}{n!}, \qquad \text{valid for } -k_A(c,x) \leq 1, \qquad (2.5)$$

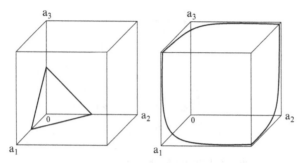

Fig. 2.9 Two examples of frontiers. *Left*: the additive frontier defined by $\alpha = a_1 + \cdots + a_n$. *Right*: the multiplicative frontier defined by $\alpha = a_1 \cdot a_2 \cdots a_n$

where n is the number of pixels in c. Notice that when $-k_A(c,x) = a_1 + \cdots + a_n > 1$ the previous formula is no longer valid because part of the simplex lays outside the hypercube, overestimating the volume; for this same reason, (2.5) is always an upper bound to the probability term and

$$N_{\text{tests}} \frac{(a_1 + \cdots + a_n)^n}{n!} \leq \varepsilon$$

implies an ε-meaningful detection, even if it is not a necessary condition. A closed-form expression valid for any value of $k_A(c,x)$ can be derived from the general case of hypercube and half-plane intersections given in [59]:

$$\mathbb{P}[k_A(c,X) \geq k_A(c,x)] = \frac{1}{n!} \sum_{i=0}^{\lfloor -k_A(c,x) \rfloor} (-1)^i \binom{n}{i} [-k_A(c,x) - i]^n ,$$

where $\lfloor -k_A(c,x) \rfloor$ is the largest integer not greater than $-k_A(c,x)$. Notice that (2.5) corresponds to the first term of this sum.

For the multiplicative case we need to observe that since the values a_j are uniformly distributed under H_0, $-\log(a_j)$ follows an exponential distribution under H_0 and $k_M(c,X)$ a Γ distribution with parameters $(n, 1)$. There is a simple closed form for the associated cumulative distribution function $\mathbb{P}[k_M(c,X) \geq k_M(c,x)]$:

Proposition 3.

$$\mathbb{P}[k_M(c,X) \geq k_M(c,x)] = \exp\left(-k_M(c,x)\right) e_{n-1}\left(k_M(c,x)\right) ,$$

where $e_m(z) = 1 + z + \frac{z^2}{2} + \cdots + \frac{z^m}{m!}$.

Proof. The density of a Γ distribution of parameters $(n, 1)$ has the form, $\frac{t^{n-1}}{(n-1)!} e^{-t}$. Hence

$$\mathbb{P}[k_M(c,X) \geq k_M(c,x)] = \frac{1}{(n-1)!} \int_{k_M(c,x)}^{+\infty} t^{n-1} e^{-t} dt .$$

Integration by parts leads to the sought formula. $\square$

Fig. 2.10 Line segment detection for the image shown in Fig. 1.1, using continuous angular precision with additive (*left*) and multiplicative (*right*) NFA. Both results are very similar to the one obtained with a multi-precision p approach (Fig. 1.1)

For both, the additive and the multiplicative methods, the candidates that satisfy the test $\text{NFA}(c,x) \leq \varepsilon$ are selected as detections and we set $\varepsilon = 1$ as usual. Figure 2.10 shows sample detections for both criteria. Comparing with Fig. 1.1, one can see that the discrete formulation produces comparable results, but requires a multi-precision p approach. Among the continuous formulations, the additive criterion seems to capture slightly finer details.

2.6 Exclusion Principle and Further Improvements

As illustrated in Fig. 2.5, an exhaustive search for line segments produces many redundant detections. Two divergent approaches were proposed to cope with redundancy and inaccuracy. The first one uses a criterion to select the best detections and remove the others; this is done *after* the exhaustive search and validation. The second one uses the *heuristic search plus validation* strategy where a reduced number of candidates is selected *previously* to validation.

Desolneux, Moisan, Morel and Almansa proposed various criteria to cope with redundancy [4, 5, 19–22]. Only the *exclusion principle* [22] will be described here, the most general of them. With a name borrowed from *quantum mechanics*, the principle is defined as follows:

Definition 3 (Exclusion Principle). Each measurement can support (or vote for) at most one detection.

In the case of line segment detection, *measurements* refer to level-line angles; in other words, each pixel of the image can vote for only one final line segment. The previous general definition does not indicate how a measurement should choose the candidate to vote. An iterative algorithm is generally used:

Algorithm 1: Exclusion principle

---

input: An set of candidates $\mathscr{C}$.
output: A list $\mathscr{O}$ of detections.

1 Mark all pixels as **Available**.
2 Select the candidate $c \in \mathscr{C}$ with best (smallest) $\mathrm{NFA}(c)$ value.
3 **while** $\mathrm{NFA}(c) \leq \varepsilon$ **do**
4   Add c to $\mathscr{O}$ and remove it from $\mathscr{C}$.
5   Mark the aligned pixels in c as **Unavailable**.
6   Recompute all NFA values counting *only* **Available** pixels.
7   Select $c \in \mathscr{C}$ with best (smallest) $\mathrm{NFA}(c)$ value.
8 **end**

Fig. 2.11 Redundancy reduction by Exclusion Principle. *Left*: input image. *Center*: all meaningful line segments. *Right*: meaningful line segments using the exclusion principle

The line segment with the smallest NFA value will be selected first and it will usually correspond well to a straight edge on the image. Then, all its aligned pixels are *excluded* from being used by the remaining candidates, whose NFA values are re-computed without using them. Redundant detections share most of their aligned pixels. Thus, when the best candidate appropriates its pixels, it leaves few or no aligned pixels on redundant line segments; the new NFA values are large and the redundant line segments are no longer meaningful. Figure 2.11 shows an example.

Unfortunately, the previous approach does not solve all the problems. When two or more aligned line segments are present, see Fig. 2.12, the exclusion principle can provide an erroneous interpretation: a longer structure covering all the aligned ones may be preferred to individual detections. For example, imagine that the level-line field shown in Fig. 2.13 appears in a 100×100 image. With a precision $p = 1/32$, the NFA value for each line segment of six elements is $100^4 \cdot 32^{-6} \approx 0.09$. The longer line segment covering the full 18 pixels has 12 aligned pixels, and its NFA

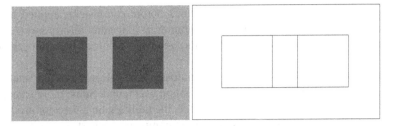

Fig. 2.12 The problem of aligned structures. *Left*: an image of two aligned squares. *Right*: meaningful line segments using the exclusion principle

Fig. 2.13 Which is the best interpretation for these level-line elements: *two* line segments, each of six elements, or *one* longer line segment of 18 elements?

values is $100^4 \cdot B(18,12,1/32) \approx 10^{-5.9}$. When comparing individual line segments, the long one has a better (smaller) NFA value than each of the shorter ones; thus one long line segment results from the exclusion principle.

Now, the two interpretations were not compared fairly. The data sets were of different size: 6 against 18 observed pixels. More reasonable would be to compare the interpretation of the entire data as *one* long line segment against the interpretation of *two* aligned line segments. This idea is used in the *multisegment detector* [31, 34]. The input digital image is analyzed line by line in all directions, and for each line the best interpretation in terms of aligned line segments is computed. A set of aligned and disjoint line segments will be called a multisegment, see Fig. 2.14.

Each line of an image is analyzed as a binary sequence of aligned or not aligned pixels (given a precision p). Then, every binary segmentation of the sequence is considered and its quality is evaluated by the NFA of an n-multisegment $(s_1, \ldots, s_n)$ supported by the line L:

$$\mathrm{NFA}(s_1, \ldots, s_n) = \#\mathscr{L} \cdot \binom{l(L)}{2n} \cdot \prod_{i=1}^{n} \left(l(s_i) + 1\right) B\left(l(s_i), k(s_i), p\right),$$

where $\#\mathscr{L}$ stands for the total number of lines considered on the image, $l(L)$ and $l(s_i)$ stand for the length of the line L and of the line segment s_i, respectively, and $k(s_i)$ is the number of aligned pixels on the line segment s_i. A multisegment $(s_1, \ldots, s_n)$ is called ε-meaningful whenever $\mathrm{NFA}(s_1, \ldots, s_n) \leq \varepsilon$. The multisegment with the lowest NFA value gives the best interpretation for that line. Actually, the core of the multisegment detector, including the NFA definition stated before, works as a general-purpose binary sequence segmentation algorithm and can be used for other problems as well.

A multi-precision p approach as described before can also be applied to the multisegment detector and a dynamic programming algorithm allows some speed improvements. Refer to [31, 34] for a thorough description of the multisegment detector.

Figure 2.15 shows the result of the multisegment detector for the image in Fig. 2.12. As one can see, the right interpretation was found. Some more examples will be commented in Chap. 4. As we will see, the multisegment detector produces, in general, satisfactory results. The algorithm computes the best interpretation for each line. Nevertheless, the best interpretation *line by line* does not always correspond to the best *global* interpretation of the image. Figure 2.16 shows an example. The method can be extended even further in this sense, preferring the best interpretation in terms of line segments for the whole image. The formulation would be necessarily much more complex, carrying the implicit suggestion of further extensions to incorporate other geometrical structures in the global interpretation.

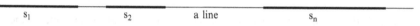

s_1 s_2 a line s_n

Fig. 2.14 An n-multisegment is an n-tuple $(s_1, \ldots, s_n)$ of n *disjoint* and *collinear* line segments

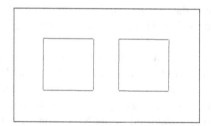

Fig. 2.15 The result of the multisegment detector on the example of Fig. 2.12

The multisegment detector is so far the more sophisticated line segment detector in the family of *a contrario* exhaustive methods. The *exhaustive* approach leads nonetheless to inefficient algorithms: the original method has an algorithmic complexity of $O(N^4)$, for an $N \times N$ image, whereas the multisegment detector has a complexity of $O(N^5)$. These algorithms could hardly produce *real time* results and their computation time is prohibitive even for medium size images.

The next chapter describes the alternative approach, the heuristic search plus validation used in the LSD algorithm.

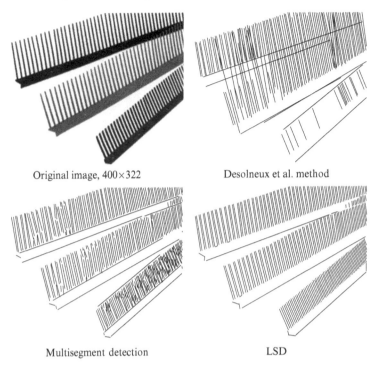

Original image, 400×322	Desolneux et al. method

Multisegment detection	LSD

Fig. 2.16 A comparison between three *a contrario* line segment detection methods. Desolneux et al. and the multisegment detector, both hallucinate global structures as a result of the aligned combs. Desolneux et al. produces slanted and longer detections. The multisegment detector makes erroneous cuts in line segments and some slanted ones

Chapter 3
The LSD Algorithm

This chapter describes in full detail the LSD algorithm [31, 35, 36] for line segment detection. It is based on the *a contrario* framework described in the previous chapter, but instead of searching exhaustively for line segments, it uses the *heuristic search plus validation* approach, resulting in an efficient algorithm. The source code and an online demo for LSD are available at [36].

3.1 Main Ideas

LSD combines a heuristic line segment search algorithm with an *a contrario* validation method. The heuristic is based on the algorithm by Burns, Hanson, and Riseman [13] that extracts line segments in three steps:

1. Partition the image into *line-support regions*, see Fig. 3.1;
2. Compute a rectangular approximation for each line-support region;
3. Validate.

Fig. 3.1 An image (*left*), the level-line field (*center*), and three line-support regions (*right*). (The level-line element arrowheads were not drawn here)

R. Grompone von Gioi, *A Contrario Line Segment Detection*, SpringerBriefs in Computer Science, DOI 10.1007/978-1-4939-0575-1_3, © The Author(s) 2014

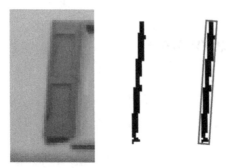

Fig. 3.2 An image (*left*), a line-support region (*center*), and its rectangle approximation (*right*)

The core of LSD follows this three-step structure too, incorporating several additions and modifications that will be described later. But the main difference is in step 3, where an *a contrario* validation step is used.

LSD starts by computing the level-line angle at each pixel to produce a *level-line field*, i.e., a unit vector field such that all vectors are tangent to the level-line going through their base point. Then, this field is segmented into connected regions of pixels that share the same level-line angle up to a certain tolerance τ. These connected regions are called *line-support regions*, see Fig. 3.1. The method used to compute the line-support regions in LSD differs from the one used by Burns et al. and will be described in Sect. 3.7.

Each line-support region (a set of pixels) is a candidate for a line segment and the corresponding geometrical object (a rectangle in this case) must be associated with it, see Fig. 3.2. The principal inertial axis of the line-support region is used as the main rectangle direction; the size of the rectangle is chosen to cover the complete region. This step is described in Sect. 3.8.

Finally, the validation step follows the same ideas described in Sect. 2.2. According to Definition 2, the pixels in the rectangle whose level-line angles correspond to the angle of the rectangle up to a tolerance τ are called *aligned pixels*. The total number of pixels in the rectangle, n, and its number of aligned pixels, k, are counted and used to validate or not the rectangle as a detected *line segment*, see Fig. 3.3.

The heuristic method solves two problems at the same time. First, it makes the algorithm fast, being able to compute the result in linear time relative to the number of pixels, see Sects. 3.12 and 4.5. The algorithmic complexity is $O(N^2)$ for an $N \times N$ image, instead of $O(N^4)$ or $O(N^5)$ for the exhaustive approaches, as discussed in the previous chapter. Second, the heuristic solves the problem of redundancy: the candidates tested are line-support regions, resulting from a particular *segmentation* of the input image; as a consequence, line segment candidates cannot overlap. For this reason, LSD does not produce redundant detections. Nevertheless, the considered heuristic does not always select the best candidate, and may result in the partition of one line segment into many of them. If strong noise is present, it may even fail to propose a candidate and meaningful line segments be lost. These cases are analyzed in Sects. 3.10 and 4.2.

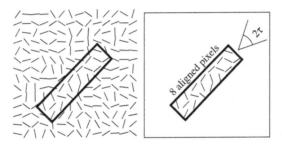

Fig. 3.3 *Left*: a rectangle candidate superposed over the level-line field. *Right*: the rectangle counts eight aligned pixels among 20. (The level-line element arrowheads were not drawn here)

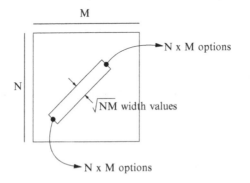

Fig. 3.4 Estimation of the number of tests

The *a contrario* formulation is very similar to the one presented in Sect. 2.2. The same *a contrario* stochastic model H_0 is used. The main difference is that now the width of the rectangles is derived from the line-support regions instead of being fixed to one; compare Figs. 2.4 and 3.3. Here we will denote the candidates by r and the set of all candidates by $\mathscr{R}$ to emphasize that they correspond to *rectangles*.

The variable width of rectangles needs to be considered in the count of the number of tests. For each of the $NM \times NM$ different line segments in an $N \times M$ image, we will count $\sqrt{NM}$ different width values, see Fig. 3.4. This is a slight overestimation, but what is relevant is the order of magnitude. LSD uses a multi-precision p approach as described in Sect. 2.4. Then, the number γ of different p values also needs to be included in the number of tests. Finally,

$$N_{\text{tests}} = (NM)^{5/2}\gamma .$$

Given an image x and a candidate rectangle r, the number of aligned pixels will be denoted by $k(r,x)$, while $n(r)$ is the total number of pixels in r.

$$\text{NFA}(r,x) = N_{\text{tests}} \cdot \mathbb{P}[k(r,X) \geq k(r,x)] ,$$

where X is a random image following H_0. Replacing the number of tests and the binomial tail for the probability term we get:

$$\text{NFA}(r,x) = (NM)^{5/2}\gamma \cdot B\Big(n(r),k(r,x),p\Big) \,. \tag{3.1}$$

A threshold ε is selected and rectangle candidates with $\text{NFA}(r,x) \leq \varepsilon$ are the detections of the algorithm. The formulation is the same as before and Proposition 2 is still valid, so the detections are called ε-*meaningful rectangles*.

Considering that in practice only the line-support regions found by the heuristic are tested, one may be tempted to set N_{tests} equal to the number of line-support regions effectively found. That could be possible, but it would imply to change the *a contrario* stochastic model. The reason is that in LSD the tests are selected as the bounding boxes of connected regions of pixels *sharing* the same level-line orientation. Then, even if the input image follows H_0, the pixels inside these bounding boxes will not: due to the line-support region algorithm, their statistics would be far from isotropic. A different H_0 could be proposed to consider this, but the complexity of the task makes it hardly worthy; it is simpler to keep the validation as if all the tests were made and the heuristic just suggests how to skip many of them.

3.2 The Complete LSD Algorithm

The previous section provided an overview of the LSD algorithm, describing its more important aspects. But there are many more details to be considered. We will see here a complete description of LSD and the rest of this chapter will describe each step in full detail. Algorithm 2 is a pseudocode for the full algorithm.

The algorithm takes an image as input and produces a list of rectangles, the detected line segments. The first step performs an image down-scaling to cope with some quantization problems, as will be discussed in Sect. 3.3. This step requires the *scale* factor and the filtering kernel size σ.

The second step computes the gradient at each pixel of the scaled-down image. The result is threefold: the level-line field λ, the gradient magnitude $|\nabla x|$ at each pixel and a list of image pixels, ordered according to their gradient magnitude. This computation is described in Sects. 3.4 and 3.5.

LSD is a greedy algorithm. A Status variable is assigned to each pixel to keep track of the ones still "Available" to form line-support regions and the ones already used or discarded, thus "Unavailable". Step 3 discards all the pixels whose gradient magnitude is less than or equal to ρ, rejecting image flat zones and pixels highly affected by quantization noise, see Sect. 3.6.

Line-support regions are obtained by a region growing algorithm, step 6. Starting from a seed pixel P, neighbor pixels are iteratively added if their level-line angles correspond to the one of the region up to a tolerance τ. As pixels are added to the region, their Status is set to "Unavailable" to prevent them from being used again. This process is described in Sect. 3.7. Pixels with large gradient magnitude

---

Algorithm 2: LSD: line segment detector

---

input: An image x.

output: A list *out* of rectangles.

1   $x_S \leftarrow \text{ScaleImage}(x, scale, \sigma)$

2   $(\lambda, |\nabla x_S|, \text{OrderedListPixels}) \leftarrow \text{Gradient}(x_S)$

3   $\text{Status} \leftarrow \begin{cases} \text{Unavailable}, & \text{pixels with } |\nabla x_S| \leq \rho \\ \text{Available}, & \text{otherwise} \end{cases}$

4   **foreach** *pixel* $P \in \text{OrderedListPixels}$ **do**

5 | **if** $\text{Status}(P) = \text{Available}$ **then**

6 | | $region \leftarrow \text{RegionGrow}(P, \tau)$

7 | | $rect \leftarrow \text{Rectangle}(region)$

8 | | **while** $\text{AlignedPixelDensity}(rect, \tau) < D$ **do**

9 | | | $region \leftarrow \text{CutRegion}(region)$

10 | | | $rect \leftarrow \text{Rectangle}(region)$

11 | | **end**

12 | | $rect \leftarrow \text{ImproveRectangle}(rect)$

13 | | $nfa \leftarrow \text{NFA}(rect, \tau)$

14 | | **if** $nfa \leq \varepsilon$ **then**

15 | | | **Add** *rect* to *out*

16 | | **end**

17 | **end**

18   **end**

---

are generally better centered along edges; thus, the seed pixels P are selected from OrderedListPixels starting with the ones with larger gradient magnitude, step 4.

The computation of the rectangle corresponding to a line-support region, steps 7 and 10, is described in Sect. 3.8. A low density of aligned pixels in the rectangle usually reveals a line-support region that is not locally straight. In such cases, step 8, the region is cut until the density attains a value of at least D, see Sect. 3.10. In some cases, some simple variations of the initial rectangle can improve the detectability, step 12. Section 3.11 describes the variations tried.

Section 3.9 discusses the computation of the NFA value and the threshold ε. Finally, Sect. 3.12 gives an analysis of the computational complexity of the LSD algorithm.

LSD was designed as an automatic image analysis tool. As such, it must work without requiring any parameter tuning. The algorithm actually depends on several quantities that determine its behavior; but their values were carefully devised to work on all images. They are therefore part of LSD's design, *internal* parameters, and are not left to the user's choice. Changing their values would amount to define a new variant of the algorithm, in the same way as we could make variants by changing the gradient operator or the region growing algorithm.

The six internal parameters of LSD are: *scale*, σ, ρ, τ, D, and ε. The following sections will describe in detail each step of LSD, commenting in each case on the internal parameters involved and the criteria used to select their values.

3.3 Image Scaling

The result of LSD is different when the image is analyzed at different scales or
if the algorithm is applied only to a small part of the image. This is natural and
corresponds to the different details that one can see when an image is observed
from a certain distance or if attention is paid to a specific part. As a result of the *a
contrario* validation step, the detection thresholds automatically adapt to the image
size. The user can select the scale of analysis by zooming or cropping the image
beforehand. Otherwise, LSD processes the entire input image as follows.

The first step of LSD is to scale the input image to 80 % of its size. This scaling
helps to cope with aliasing and quantization artifacts (especially the staircase effect)
present in many images. Blurring the image would produce the same effect but affect
the statistics of the image; some structures would be detected on blurred white noise.
But when correctly sub-sampled, the white noise statistics are preserved. Note that
the *a contrario* validation is applied to the scaled down image. Thus, the $N \times M$
image size that appears in the number of tests included in the NFA computation
corresponds to an input image of size $1.25N \times 1.25M$.

Figure 3.5 shows two discrete edges at different angles, both presenting the staircase effect. Next to each image is the result of LSD without using the initial scaling
(center). In the first case the edge is detected as four horizontal line segments instead
of one; in the second case, no line segment is detected. In both cases the result is
reasonable, but it does not correspond to what we would expect. Figure 3.5 (right)
shows the result of LSD using the 80 % scaling. Both edges are now detected and
with the right orientation (even if the first one is still fragmented).

The scale factor of 80 % (*scale* = 0.8), is the smallest image reduction that reasonably solves the staircase problem while producing almost the same result as a
full scale analysis on images without artifacts. (An 80 % scaling means here that the
numbers of rows and columns are both reduced to 80 %; the number of pixels is thus
reduced to 64 %.)

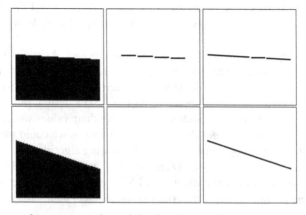

Fig. 3.5 Discrete edges at two angles and the detections with and without scaling. *Left*: input
images, 100×100 pixels. *Center*: detection without scaling. *Right*: detection with scaling

The scaling is performed by a Gaussian sub-sampling: the image is filtered with a Gaussian kernel to avoid aliasing and then it is sub-sampled. The standard deviation of the Gaussian kernel is determined by $\sigma = \Sigma/scale$, where $scale$ is the scaling factor. The value of Σ is set to 0.6, which gives a good balance between avoiding aliasing and limiting image blurring.

An alternative way of avoiding aliasing and quantization artifacts is to use a blurred version but at full scale of the input image to generate candidates, while still using the original input image for the *a contrario* validation. Blurring the image does affect its statistics, as mentioned before, but it is irrelevant if it is only used for candidate selection. On the other hand, the staircase effect and part of the noise are removed by blurring and the region growing process can produce better candidates. This strategy is not used in the LSD algorithm.

3.4 Gradient Computation

Let $x(u,v)$ denote the image gray level value at pixel (u,v). The image gradient $\nabla x = (g_u, g_v)$ at each pixel is approximated by a 2×2 operator:

$$g_u(u,v) = \frac{x(u+1,v) + x(u+1,v+1) - x(u,v) - x(u,v+1)}{2},$$

$$g_v(u,v) = \frac{x(u,v+1) + x(u+1,v+1) - x(u,v) - x(u+1,v)}{2}.$$

The level-line angle is computed as

$$\lambda(u,v) = \arctan\left(\frac{g_u(u,v)}{-g_v(u,v)}\right)$$

and the gradient magnitude as

$$|\nabla x(u,v)| = \sqrt{g_u^2(u,v) + g_v^2(u,v)}.$$

This simple scheme uses the smallest possible mask size in its computation, thus reducing as much as possible the dependence of the computed gradient values and approaching the theoretical independence in the case of a noisy image. Based on the arguments of Sect. 2.3, we will assume that the computed angle values are independent.

The level-line angles encode the direction of the edge, that is, the angle of the dark to light transition. Note that a dark to light transition and a light to dark transition are different, having a 180 degrees angle difference between the corresponding gradient or level-line angles. This means that the resulting line segments detected by LSD are oriented and that the order of their starting and ending points is not arbitrary, since it encodes which side of the line segment is darker. For example, if the contrast of an image is reversed (changing black to white and white to black) the result of LSD would be the same, but the starting and ending points would be exchanged on every line segment.

The previous formulas compute an approximation of the image gradient at coordinates $(u + 0.5, v + 0.5)$ and not (u, v). This half-pixel offset is then added to the output of LSD to the rectangles' coordinates to produce coherent results.

3.5 Gradient Pseudo-Ordering

LSD is a greedy algorithm and the order in which pixels are processed has an impact on the result. Pixels with high gradient magnitude correspond to more contrasted edges. In an edge, the central pixels usually have the highest gradient magnitude. So it makes sense to start looking for line segments at pixels with the highest gradient magnitude.

Sorting algorithms usually require $O(n \log n)$ operations to sort n values. However, a simple pixel pseudo-ordering is possible in linear time. To this aim, 1024 bins are created corresponding to equal gradient magnitude intervals between zero and the largest observed value for gradient magnitude on the image. Pixels are classified into the bins according to their gradient magnitude. LSD uses first seed pixels from the bin with the largest gradient magnitudes; then it takes seed pixels from the second bin, and so on until exhaustion of all bins. 1024 bins are enough to sort almost strictly the gradient values when the gray level values are quantized in the integer range [0,255].

3.6 Gradient Threshold

Pixels with small gradient magnitude correspond to flat zones or slow gradients. Also, they naturally present a higher error in the gradient computation due to the quantization of their values. In LSD, the pixels with gradient magnitude smaller than ρ are therefore rejected and not used in the construction of line-support regions or rectangles.

Assuming a quantization noise n and an ideal image x, we observe

$$\tilde{x} = x + n \qquad \nabla \tilde{x} = \nabla x + \nabla n .$$

From Fig. 3.6, we have

$$|\text{angle error}| \leq \arcsin\left(\frac{q}{|\nabla x|}\right) ,$$

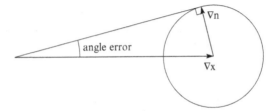

Fig. 3.6 Estimation of the angle error due to quantization noise

where q is a bound on $|\nabla n|$. The criterion used is to reject pixels where the angle error is larger than the angle tolerance τ used in the region growing algorithm. That is, we impose $|\text{angle error}| \leq \tau$ and we get

$$\rho = \frac{q}{\sin \tau}.$$

The threshold ρ is set using the last expression where q is a bound on the possible error in the gradient value due to quantization effects [35], and τ is the angle tolerance to be used in the region growing algorithm.

In the usual case, the pixel values are quantized to integer values in $\{0, 1, \ldots, 255\}$. Thus, the maximal possible error in the gradient is 1 (when adjacent pixels have quantization errors of 0.5 that do not compensate). For empirical reasons, we preferred a more conservative bound and we set $q = 2$. This value will not, however, give good results if the image intensity range differs significantly from the [0,255] interval.

3.7 Region Growing

Starting from a pixel in the ordered list of available pixels—the seed—a region growing algorithm is applied to form a line-support region. Recursively, the available neighbors of the pixels already in the region are tested, and the ones whose

Fig. 3.7 Iterative growing of a line-support region. The level-line orientation field (orthogonal to the gradient orientation field) is represented by *dashes*. Marked pixels are the ones forming the region. From *left* to *right*: first, second, third iterations and final result. (The level-line element arrowheads were not drawn here)

level-line angle is equal to the *region angle* θ_{region} up to a tolerance τ are added to the region, see Fig. 3.7. The initial region angle θ_{region} is set to the level-line angle of the seed pixel, and each time a new pixel is added to the region, the region angle value is updated to

$$\arctan\left(\frac{\sum_j \sin(\text{level-line-angle}_j)}{\sum_j \cos(\text{level-line-angle}_j)}\right),$$

where the index j runs over the pixels in the region. If we associate to each pixel in the region a unitary vector with its level-line angle, the last formula corresponds to the angle of the mean vector. The process is repeated until no other pixel can be added to the region. Algorithm 3 gives a precise description of the region growing step.

Algorithm 3: RegionGrow

    input : A level-line field λ, a initial pixel *Seed*, an angle tolerance τ, and a Status variable
             for each pixel.
    output: A set of pixels: *region*.

1 **Add** *Seed* to *region*
2 $\theta_{region} \leftarrow \lambda(Seed)$
3 $S_x \leftarrow \cos(\theta_{region})$
4 $S_y \leftarrow \sin(\theta_{region})$
5 **foreach** *pixel* $P \in region$ **do**
6   **foreach** *pixel* $Q \in$ Neighborhood(P) **and** Status$(Q) =$ Available **do**
7   **if** AngleDiff$(\theta_{region}, \lambda(Q)) \leq \tau$ **then**
8   **Add** Q to *region*
9   Status$(Q) \leftarrow$ Unavailable.
10               $S_x \leftarrow S_x + \cos(\lambda(Q))$
11               $S_y \leftarrow S_y + \sin(\lambda(Q))$
12               $\theta_{region} \leftarrow \arctan(S_y/S_x)$.
13   **end**
14   **end**
15 **end**

An 8-connected neighborhood is used, so the neighbors of pixel $x(u,v)$ are $x(u-1,v-1), x(u,v-1), x(u+1,v-1), x(u-1,v), x(u+1,v), x(u-1,v+1), x(u,v+1)$, and $x(u+1,v+1)$.

The tolerance τ is set to 22.5 degrees ($\pi/8$ radians), which corresponds to a total range of 45 degrees or $1/8$ of the full range of orientations. It was chosen because it is about the largest possible range where it is still reasonable to call a pixel "oriented like the rectangle". What is important is not the exact value but the order of magnitude, so it was set to obtain $p = 1/8$. Figure 3.8 shows a typical example: on the left we see a detail of a noisy edge; next to it is the result of the

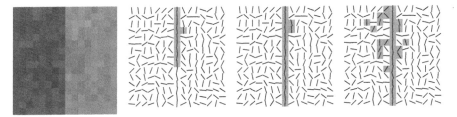

Fig. 3.8 Examples of line-support regions obtained starting at the *top center* pixel for three values of the angle tolerance. From *left* to *right*: image; $\tau = 11.25$; $\tau = 22.5$; $\tau = 45$. (The level-line element arrowheads were not drawn here)

region growing algorithm for τ set to 11.25, 22.5, and 45 degrees, respectively. The first case is too restrictive and the region obtained is too small; with 45 degrees, regions often expand too far from the edge; 22.5 is a good compromise. Regions that could be obtained with a smaller value of τ are also obtained in this way. In the validation process, smaller values of the precision p are also tested, so the value of τ only affects the region growing algorithm and not the validation.

3.8 Rectangular Approximation

A line segment corresponds to a geometrical event, a rectangle. Before evaluating a line-support region, the rectangle associated with it must be found. The region of pixels is interpreted as a solid object and the gradient magnitude of each pixel is used as the "mass" of that point. Then, the center of mass of the region is selected as the center of the rectangle and the main direction of the rectangle is set to the first inertia axis of the region. Finally, the width and length of the rectangle are set to the smallest values that make the rectangle to cover the full line-support region.

The center of the rectangle (c_u, c_v) is set to

$$c_u = \frac{\sum_{j \in region} |\nabla x(j)| \cdot u(j)}{\sum_{j \in region} |\nabla x(j)|}, \qquad c_v = \frac{\sum_{j \in region} |\nabla x(j)| \cdot v(j)}{\sum_{j \in region} |\nabla x(j)|},$$

where $|\nabla x(j)|$ is the gradient magnitude of pixel j, and the index j runs over the pixels in the region. The main rectangle's angle is set to the angle of the eigenvector associated with the smallest eigenvalue of the matrix

$$M = \begin{pmatrix} m^{uu} & m^{uv} \\ m^{uv} & m^{vv} \end{pmatrix}$$

with

$$m^{uu} = \frac{\sum_{j \in region} |\nabla x(j)| \cdot (u(j) - c_u)^2}{\sum_{j \in region} |\nabla x(j)|},$$

$$m^{vv} = \frac{\sum_{j \in region} |\nabla x(j)| \cdot (v(j) - c_v)^2}{\sum_{j \in region} |\nabla x(j)|},$$

$$m^{uv} = \frac{\sum_{j \in region} |\nabla x(j)| \cdot (u(j) - c_u)(v(j) - c_v)}{\sum_{j \in region} |\nabla x(j)|}.$$

3.9 NFA Computation

The *a contrario* validation depends on the precision p, whose value is initially set to τ/π, where τ is the angular tolerance used in the region growing algorithm. But other values are also tested as will be explained in Sect. 3.11; a total of γ different values for p are tried. The total number of pixels in the rectangle is denoted by n and the number of p-aligned pixels is denoted by k (we drop r and x when they are implicit to simplify the notation). Then, the number of false alarms (NFA) associated with the rectangle r is

$$NFA(r) = (NM)^{5/2} \gamma \cdot B(n, k, p),$$

where N and M are the number of columns and rows of the image (after scaling), and $B(n, k, p)$ is the tail of the binomial distribution,

$$B(n, k, p) = \sum_{j=k}^{n} \binom{n}{j} p^j (1 - p)^{n-j}.$$

All in all, for each rectangle being evaluated and given a precision p, the numbers k and n are counted, and then the NFA value is computed by

$$NFA(r) = (NM)^{5/2} \gamma \cdot \sum_{j=k}^{n} \binom{n}{j} p^j (1 - p)^{n-j}. \tag{3.2}$$

The rectangles with $NFA(r) \leq \varepsilon$ are validated as detections.

As stated before and following Desolneux, Moisan, and Morel [19, 22], we set $\varepsilon = 1$ once for all. Here we will only show an experiment illustrating the stability of the result relative to ε value. Figure 3.9 shows the input image and the result of LSD with $\varepsilon = 1$, $\varepsilon = 10^{-1}$, and $\varepsilon = 10^{-2}$, respectively. Only a few small line segments mark a difference between the three results.

Fig. 3.9 Result of LSD for the image on the *left* for three different ε values: $\varepsilon = 1$, $\varepsilon = 10^{-1}$, and $\varepsilon = 10^{-2}$

3.10 Aligned Pixel Density

In some cases, the τ-angle tolerance region growing method produces a wrong interpretation. This problem arises when two straight edges form an obtuse angle near 180 degree. Figure 3.10 shows an example of a line-support region (in gray) and the rectangle corresponding to it. This line-support region could be better interpreted as two thinner rectangles, one longer than the other, forming an obtuse angle. As these two thin rectangles are aligned one to the other up to a tolerance τ, all the pixels of both rectangles are grouped into one line-support region.

In LSD this problem is handled by detecting problematic line-support regions and cutting them into two smaller regions, hoping to cut the region at the right place to solve the problem. The criterion is described below. Once a region is cut, if the new one is accepted, the rectangle associated is recomputed and the algorithm is resumed.

The detection of this "angle problem" is based on the density of aligned pixels in the rectangle. When the problem is not present, the rectangle matches well the line-support region and the density of aligned pixels is high. When the "angle problem" is present, as can be seen in Fig. 3.10, the density of aligned pixels is low. Also, when a slightly curved edge is being locally approximated by a sequence of straight edges, the degree of the approximation (how many line segments are used to approximate the curve) is related to the density of aligned pixels.

The density of aligned pixels of a rectangle is computed as the ratio of the number of aligned pixels (k in the previous notation) to the area of the rectangle:

$$d = \frac{k}{\text{length}(r) \cdot \text{width}(r)} \ .$$

A threshold D is defined and rectangles should have a density d larger than or equal to D to be accepted. We set D to the value 0.7 (70 %) which provides good balance between solving the "angle problem", providing smooth approximations to curves, and without over-cutting true line segments.

Fig. 3.10 A problem that can arise in the region growing process: a particular line-support region (*gray*) and the rectangle assigned to it

Two methods for cutting the region are actually tried: *reducing the angle tolerance* and *reducing the region radius*. In both methods part of the pixels in the region are kept while the others are re-marked again as Available, so they can be used again in future line-support regions. We will describe now these two methods.

The first method, *reducing the angle tolerance*, tries to guess a new angle tolerance τ' that adapts well to the region, and then the region growing algorithm is used again with the same seed but using the newly estimated tolerance value. When two straight regions that form an obtuse angle are present, this method is expected to get the tolerance that would get only one of these two regions, the one containing the seed pixel.

If all the pixels in the region were used in the estimation of the tolerance, the new value would be such that all the pixels would still be accepted. Instead, only the pixels near the seed are used. The width of the initial rectangle (the one whose aligned pixel density was too low) is used to set the neighborhood size of the seed: Only the pixels whose distance to the seed is less than the width of the initial rectangle are used. In that way, the locality of the estimation of τ' adapts to the size of the region.

All the pixels in that neighborhood of the seed point are evaluated, and the new tolerance τ' is set to twice the standard deviation of the level-line angles of these pixels. With this new value, the same region growing algorithm is applied, starting from the same seed point. Before that, all the pixels on the original regions are set to Available, so the algorithm can use them again, and the discarded ones are available for further regions.

The previous method is tried only once, and if the resulting line-support region fails to satisfy the density criterion, the second method, *reducing the region radius*, is repetitively tried. The idea of this second method is to gradually remove the pixels that are farthest from the seed until the criterion is satisfied or the region is too small and rejected. This method works best when the line-support region corresponds to a curve and the region needs to be reduced until the density criterion is satisfied, usually meaning that a certain degree of approximation to the curve is obtained.

The distance from the seed point to the farthest pixel in the region is called the *radius* of the region. Each iteration of this method removes the farthest pixels of the region to reduce the region's *radius* to 75 % of its value. This process is repeated until the density criterion is satisfied or until there are not enough pixels in the region to form a meaningful rectangle. This is just a way of gradually reducing the region until the criterion is satisfied; it could be done one pixel at a time, but that would make the process slower.

3.11 Rectangle Improvement

Before rejecting a line-support region for being not meaningful (NFA $> \varepsilon$), LSD tries some variations of the rectangle's configuration initially found with the aim to get a valid one. This extends the heuristic search to some more candidates than the ones provided by the region growing step.

The relevant factors tested are the precision p and the width of the rectangle. The initial precision used, corresponding to the region growing tolerance τ, is large enough and testing only smaller values makes sense. If the pixels are well aligned, using a finer precision will keep the same number of aligned points, but a smaller p yields a smaller (and therefore better) NFA value.

In a similar way, it only makes sense to try to reduce the rectangle's width because the initial width was chosen to cover the whole line-support region. Often, reducing the width by one pixel may reduce the number of aligned pixels by only a few units while reducing the total number of pixels by a number equal to the length of the rectangle, see Fig. 3.11. This may decrease significantly the binomial tail and therefore also the NFA.

The rectangle improvement routine of LSD consists of the following steps:

1. Try finer precisions,
2. Try to reduce width,
3. Try to reduce one side of the rectangle,
4. Try to reduce the other side of the rectangle,
5. Try even finer precisions.

If a meaningful rectangle is found (NFA $\le \varepsilon$), the improvement routine will stop after the step that found it.

Step 1 tries the following precision values: $p/2, p/4, p/8, p/16$, and $p/32$, where p is the initial precision value. The value that produces the best NFA (the smallest) value is kept.

Step 2 tries up to five times to reduce the rectangle width by 0.5 pixels. This means that the tested width values are $W, W - 0.5, W - 1, W - 1.5, W - 2$, and $W - 2.5$, where W is the initial width value. Again, the value that produces the best NFA value is kept.

Step 3 tries five times to reduce only one side of the rectangle by 0.5 pixel. This implies reducing the width of the rectangle by 0.5 pixels, but also moving the center of the rectangle by 0.25 pixels to maintain the position of the other side of the rectangle. So the tested side displacements are 0.5, 1, 1.5, 2, and 2.5 pixels. As before, the value that produces the best NFA value is kept. Step 4 does the same thing as step 3 on the other side of the rectangle.

Step 5 tries again to reduce the precision even further. This step tests the precision values $\hat{p}/2, \hat{p}/4, \hat{p}/8, \hat{p}/16$, and $\hat{p}/32$, where $\hat{p}$ is the precision at the beginning of this step. The value that produces the best NFA value is kept.

In addition to the initial precision $p = \frac{\tau}{\pi}$, five more values are potentially tested in step 1 and five more in step 5. Therefore, the constant γ used in the computation of the NFA value (3.2) is $\gamma = 11$. The range of precisions covered is from $p = \frac{\tau}{\pi}$ to

Fig. 3.11 A line-support region that would produce a rectangle larger than the optimal one

$p = \frac{\tau}{1024\pi}$ and is more than enough to consider any relevant case, the finer precision being about 0.02 degrees. Five such steps, attaining a 1 degree precision, would be enough; this refinement, however, works better sometimes before and sometimes after the width refinement, and there is no serious caveat in performing both.

3.12 Computational Complexity

Performing a Gaussian sub-sampling and computing the image gradient, both can be performed with a number of operations proportional to the number of pixels in the image. Then, pixels are pseudo-ordered by a classification into bins, an operation that can be done in linear time. The computational time of the line-support region finding algorithm is proportional to the number of visited pixels, and this number is equal to the total number of pixels in the regions plus the border pixels of each one. Thus, the number of visited pixels remains proportional to the total number of pixels of the image. The rest of the processing can be divided into two kind of tasks. For the first kind, for example summing the region mass or counting aligned pixels, the computations are proportional to the total number of pixels involved in all regions. For the second kind, like computing inertia axis or computing the NFA value from the number of aligned pixels, the processing time is proportional to the number of regions. Both the total number of pixels involved and the number of regions are at most equal to the number of pixels. All in all, LSD has an execution time proportional to the number of pixels in the image.

Chapter 4
Experiments

This chapter presents some experiments to illustrate the behavior of the *a contrario* line segment detector, indicating the good properties as well as its shortcomings. The results are compared with some existing approaches, concluding with an empirical evaluation of the algorithm computational time.

4.1 Basic Experiments

The typical behavior of the proposed line segment detector will be first illustrated using simple synthetic and natural images. Unless otherwise stated, all the experiments were performed with the LSD algorithm, available online at [36].

Figure 4.1 shows a simple synthetic image representing a molecular diagram composed mostly of line segments (left), and the line segments detected by the algorithm (right). Note that each line in the image produces *two* line segment detections: the algorithm is a straight edge detector and each white to black transition is an edge; lines in the image are composed of two edges, the white to black transition in one side being the first and the black to white transition in the other side the second. Most straight edges in the image produce line segment detections. The exceptions are the very short ones, as the base of the number "2": as explained in Chap. 2, being too short, the number of aligned pixels is not large enough to produce a detection.

Another synthetic image is shown in Fig. 4.2, this one composed of concentric circles. Strictly speaking, there is no straight edge present. However, the algorithm detects *locally* straight edges and thus the curved edges are approximated by line segments. Each line segment is detected independently from the others, and this determines that curved edges are cut into line segments in an arbitrary way. Some experiments in the next section show how noise affects the particular way in which the curve is cut, and Sect. 5.2 gives some hints on extensions to handle curves more appropriately. As before, very small structures, as the central black circle, are not detected.

R. Grompone von Gioi, *A Contrario Line Segment Detection*, SpringerBriefs in Computer Science, DOI 10.1007/978-1-4939-0575-1_4, © The Author(s) 2014

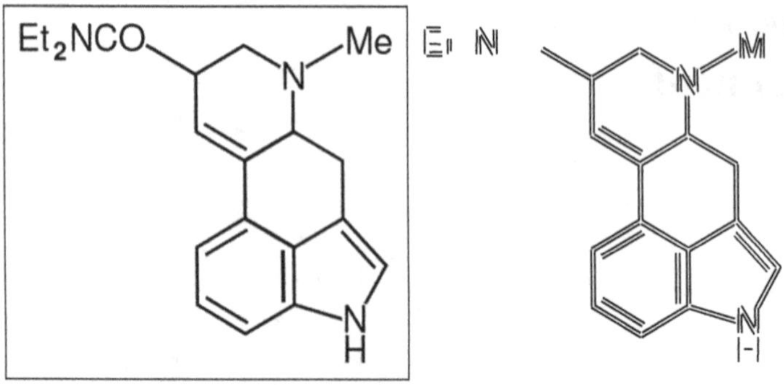

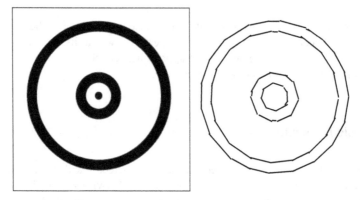

Fig. 4.1 *Left*: a synthetic image representing the molecule of lysergic acid diethylamide, 305×274 pixels. *Right*: the line segments detected by the LSD algorithm

Fig. 4.2 *Left*: a synthetic image, 249×249 pixels. *Right*: the line segments detected by the LSD algorithm

Figure 4.3 shows three experiments on natural images. The first scene contains highly geometrical content, essentially composed of flat structures with straight borders. As expected, the detected line segments represent the structure of the image well. Almost all structures are found, the perceptual exceptions being small ones that lie beyond the meaningfulness limit. In accordance with the theory, there are very few false detections. The second image shows non-geometric elements. None of the detections correspond to real straight or flat objects, they correspond to locally straight edges. An interpretation in terms of line segments is not strictly correct in the sense that hands are not straight nor flat structures, but it is a reasonable interpretation of the 2D structure present in the image at a given resolution. The line segment interpretation is only an economic approximation to a 2D curve. Such results are acceptable in the sense that every detection corresponds to a locally straight structure in the image and every locally straight structure has a line segment associated.

The last image in Fig. 4.3 shows a more complex scene. The result of the algorithm is far from perfect. And yet only the straight or locally straight structures produce detections. In general, what the current algorithm produces is a useful and compact description of the principal edges of the image.

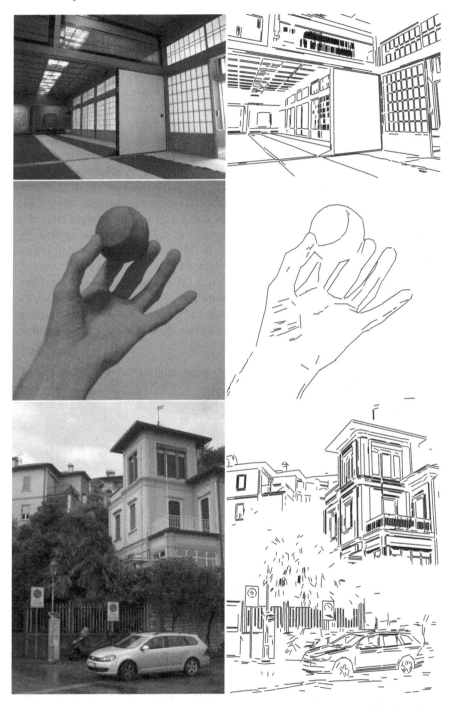

Fig. 4.3 Natural images. *Left*: input image. *Right*: line segments detected by the LSD algorithm

4.2 Noise

The LSD algorithm is composed of two steps: a heuristic search and a validation step. Both steps are affected by noise. This section focuses on its analysis.

The validation step is based on the *a contrario* framework and the *a contrario* model corresponds to white noise images. Thus, the algorithm produces few or no detections in such images. The more an image is similar to white noise, the less detections will be produced. As a result, when white noise with increasing variance is added to an image, the NFA value of an initially valid line segment increases with the noise. Eventually, noise dominates the image, the NFA becomes larger than ε, and the line segment is no longer detected.

This effect will be illustrated with a synthetic experiment. Gaussian white noise of different powers was added to an image containing a sharp straight edge at a known position. Because the position is known, the validation step is applied directly, skipping the heuristic search; this way the effect of noise on each part is analyzed separately. The NFA value is then evaluated for each noise level.

Figure 4.4 shows two such synthetic images. The initial image contains a vertical edge corresponding to a transition from gray-level 64 to 192. Noise with a standard deviation of 50 gray-levels was added to the left hand image and the line segment is still validated; on the right hand image, the added noise has a standard

Fig. 4.4 A 256×256 image containing a step from gray values 64 to 192 and altered by Gaussian white noise of standard deviation 50 (*left*) and 160 (*right*) gray-levels. The line segment at the step is meaningful (for $\varepsilon = 1$) in the left image according to the present theory (but the heuristic is not able to grow a line-support region that corresponds to it, so LSD will not detect it). Inversely, in the right hand image the noise is strong enough to mask the line segment. Refer to Fig. 4.5 to see how the NFA value varies with the noise level. The human visual system is able to see the line segment at the right image, even with a huge quantity of added noise. Nevertheless, our perception of the left image is that of a sharp edge, while the right image is perceived as a slightly blurred edge. This is compatible with the use of a multiscale analysis; if the image is analyzed at half scale, the vertical line segment corresponds to a 2 pixels width at full scale. Indeed, the line segment is meaningful at half scale, as shown in Fig. 4.6

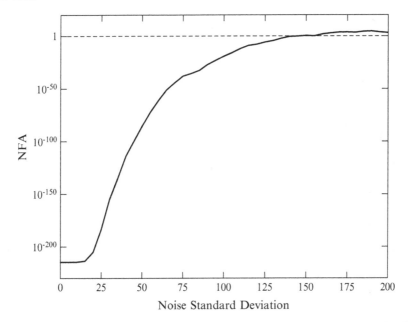

Fig. 4.5 A numerical experiment on the effect of Gaussian white noise in the NFA value. The experiment was done with step images with added noise as the ones shown in Fig. 4.4. The plot shows the NFA (in logarithmic scale) of the vertical line segment as a function of the standard deviation of the added noise. An NFA ≤ 1 indicates a meaningful line segment ($\varepsilon = 1$), while NFA > 1 corresponds to non-validated ones. Low power noise does not affect the detection. As the noise power is increased, the NFA value also gradually increases (decreasing the line segment meaningfulness). Eventually, the NFA value reaches the threshold and the line segment is no longer validated. The particular values depend on the line segment size and the relation of the edge step to the noise power. In this experiment, with a step of 128 gray-levels, the noise is negligible for $\sigma < 15$, validating the line segment with NFA $\approx 10^{-215}$. The line segment is rejected for a noise standard deviation of about $\sigma = 150$ or more

deviation of 160 gray-levels and the line segment is no longer validated. The gradual evolution of meaningfulness relative to the noise level is plotted in Fig. 4.5. The vertical axis corresponds to the NFA of the line segments, so that the smaller the value the more meaningful the line segment is; values larger than $\varepsilon = 1$ correspond to non-meaningful ones. The plot shows that low power noise does not affect the validation; then as noise power is increased, the NFA value slowly increases. In this case, noise with standard deviations of about 15 gray-levels can be neglected, while the limit of detection is when noise has a σ of about 150 gray-levels. This effect is, of course, relative to the magnitude of the step, as shown in Fig. 3.6 in Sect. 3.6. Roughly, noise can be neglected when its level is one order of magnitude smaller than the step, and the validation is precluded with noise levels of the same order of magnitude as the step. Also, short line segments require a larger proportion of aligned pixels to validate and are thus more affected.

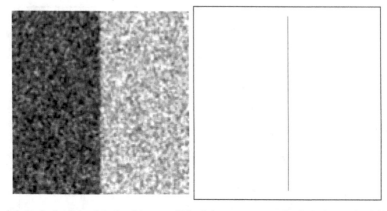

Fig. 4.6 Analysis of the right hand image of Fig. 4.4 at a coarser scale. *Left*: the result of filtering the image with a Gaussian filter of $\sigma = \sqrt{2}$ and subsampling the result by a factor 2. *Right*: At this scale the line segment is meaningful (NFA $= 10^{-55.2}$). The width of the detected line segment at this scale is 1 pixel; this corresponds, at full scale, to a line segment with a width of 2 pixels. This is in agreement with our perceptual impression of the edge as slightly blurred at the right hand image of Fig. 4.4

A criticism can be raised to the theory: the vertical line segment on the right hand image of Fig. 4.4 is not detected, even if it is perfectly visible for us. A possible answer is that the human visual system uses a multiscale analysis. For a fair comparison one must authorize the line segment detection theory to analyze the image at a different scale too. Figure 4.6 shows that the same line segment masked by noise at full scale can be detected by the very same algorithm at coarser scales. Multiscale analysis also helps in detecting global structures masked at full scale by details of the image; more on this in the next section.

The effect of noise on the heuristic search part of LSD is more critical than on the validation step. In practice this effect is dominant. Noise produces variations in the level-line angles, affecting the region growing algorithm. As for the validation step, low power noise produces negligible variations to the level-line field and the result will not be affected. Figure 4.7 shows an experiment on a synthetic image with low power Gaussian white noise. One can see that the detections are not affected by such low noise. With moderate noise power, the variations to the level-line angles become larger, occasionally reaching the angle tolerance value τ. In some cases, the region growing algorithm is not able to follow the edge and the line-support regions become fragmented. This is illustrated in Fig. 4.8, showing fragmented results, and part of line segments missing. In the presence of strong noise, the connected line-support regions found by the heuristic are very small, covering a minor part of the line segment; the validation step then rejects each of these partial parts.

The fragmentation of the line-support regions by noise happens at noise levels where the line segments would still be validated. Both images in Fig. 4.4 produce regions too fragmented and are rejected. The line segment on the left hand image, however, would be validated if the heuristic was able to find the corresponding

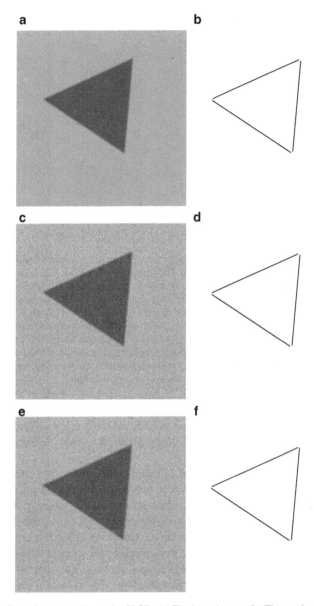

Fig. 4.7 The effect of noise on the result of LSD. (**a**) The input image. (**b**) The result of LSD shows the expected line segments. (**c**) The same image contaminated with Gaussian white noise ($\sigma = 10$). (**d**) The result of LSD on the previous image. The expected three line segments were found and the differences are negligible. (**e**) The same original image with a different realization of Gaussian white noise ($\sigma = 10$). (**f**) Again, the result is almost indistinguishable from the two previous ones. When true line segments are present in the image, LSD detects them correctly in the presence of low power Gaussian noise. (These experiments were done without the 80% image scaling described in Sect. 3.3; here we want to analyze how noise affects the region growing process, but the image filtering performed as part of the scaling would have helped the region growing algorithm)

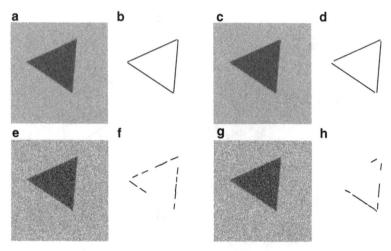

Fig. 4.8 As noise power is increased, the image is more and more similar to white noise, and the result of the LSD algorithm is degraded. (**a**) The triangle image of Fig. 4.7a with Gaussian white noise ($\sigma = 20$). (**b**) The line segments found by LSD in the previous image. (**c**) The triangle image with a different realization of Gaussian white noise ($\sigma = 20$). (**d**) The line segments found by LSD in the previous image. (**e**) The triangle image contaminated with Gaussian white noise ($\sigma = 40$). (**f**) The line segments found by LSD in the previous images. (**g**) The triangle image with a different realization of Gaussian white noise ($\sigma = 40$). (**h**) The line segments found by LSD in the previous image. (These experiments were done without the 80% image scaling described in Sect. 3.3; here we want to analyze how noise affects the region growing process, but the image filtering performed as part of the scaling would have helped the region growing algorithm)

line-support region. The heuristic used in LSD makes it a fast algorithm; the price to pay is that some line segments will not be detected, even if the underlying theory would validate them.

Noise affects the heuristic method as mentioned earlier. LSD chooses the seed pixels for the region growing algorithm by ordering the pixels according to the gradient magnitude. The noise alters the gradient magnitude; hence, it also alters the order in which seed pixels are considered. When the edges being detected are indeed straight, as in Fig. 4.7, the result is unaltered. This observation lets us verify that the growing algorithm is quite robust to the seed pixel over straight edges; roughly any pixel of the edge chosen as seed would produce the same line-support region. However, when the algorithm is growing a region over a portion of a curved edge, the particular way in which curves are cut into line segments does depend on the seed pixel. Even low noise can alter the particular approximation of curves by line segments, as shown in Fig. 4.9.

Fig. 4.9 (continued) curves by line segments, even a low-level noise can affect the particular result obtained. (The method described in Sect. 3.10 to adjust the aligned pixel density results in tight curve approximations by line segments; that step was removed in this experiment to make the dependency on the seed pixel more obvious. Also, these experiments were done without the 80% image scaling described in Sect. 3.3; here we want to analyze how noise affects the region growing process, but the image filtering performed as part of the scaling would have helped the region growing algorithm)

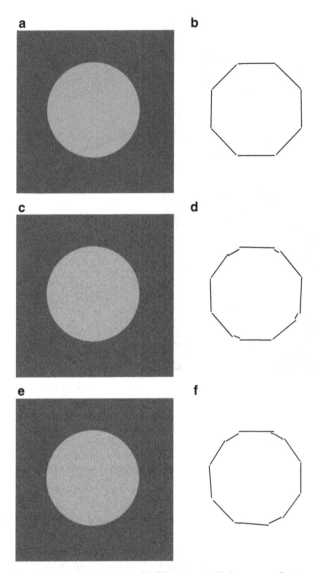

Fig. 4.9 The effect of noise in the result of LSD when applied to approximate curves by line segments. (**a**) The input image containing a circle. (**b**) The result of LSD when applied to the previous image. What we get is an almost regular approximation of the circle by line segments. The particular angle of the approximation is arbitrary and it is determined by the details of the algorithm, the fine variations in the level-line angles in the image, and the seed pixels used. In this geometric and almost perfect circle the former factor is dominant. (**c**) The same image contaminated with Gaussian white noise ($\sigma = 10$). (**d**) The line segments found by LSD in the previous image. The result is still an approximation of the circle by line segments, but an irregular one. When noise is present, the variations in the level-line angles produced by noise are the dominant factor in the determination of the particular approximation of the circle. (**e**) The same original image contaminated with a different realization of Gaussian white noise ($\sigma = 10$). (**f**) Again, we get an irregular approximation but different from the previous one. When dealing with approximations of

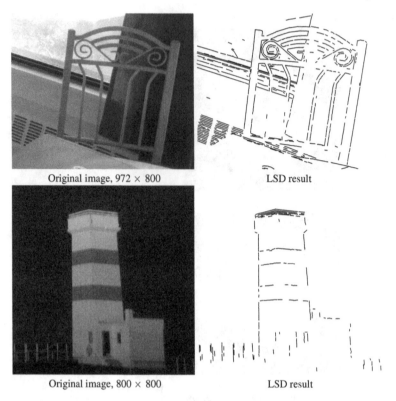

Original image, 972 × 800   LSD result

Original image, 800 × 800   LSD result

Fig. 4.10 Parts of larger photos with noise produced by the camera sensor, because of low (*top*) and very low (*bottom*) light conditions. At the right, the line segments detected by LSD. As in the synthetic examples, noise fragments line segments into small ones. (These experiments were done without the 80% image scaling described in Sect. 3.3; here we want to analyze how noise affects the region growing process, but the image filtering performed as part of the scaling would have helped the region growing algorithm)

All the results shown in this section were obtained without the initial scaling down step described in Sect. 3.3. Normally, this step reduces part of the noise, and improves the result. Indeed, the Gaussian blurring performed works as a simpler denoising step. With less level-line angle variation, the region growing process generates less fragmented regions, obtaining many valid segments that would otherwise be rejected. Of course, the improvement is obtained at the cost of reducing the resolution because a sub-sampling is needed in order for the *a contrario* independence assumption to be still valid. This can cause misdetections of short line segments, which will not have enough pixels to pass the validation test after subsampling. For this reason, it is not recommended to push further (to even lower scales) this denoising strategy. An alternative, as described in Sect. 3.3, is to generate an auxiliary blurred image to compute line-support regions, while still using the original image for the validation step.

To close this section, Fig. 4.10 shows two examples of real camera noise due to low light conditions. One can see on these images the same kind of effects that were illustrated earlier with synthetic images. There are two possible approaches to deal with images highly contaminated by noise: to use an image denoising technique, or to use a multiscale approach. Figure 4.11 shows examples of both approaches. Finally, Figs. 4.17 and 4.18 show a comparison of the results of several line segment detection methods on a noisy natural image at different scales.

4.3 Scale and Resolution

This section analyzes some of the reasons leading to unexpected interpretations of images by LSD. First, LSD detects locally straight *edges*. Yet, images often have *other* kinds of straight features; even if for humans they produce perceptual impressions of line segments, the LSD algorithm will be unable to detect them. Figure 4.12 shows a trivial dot pattern example. Most people would describe the pattern as a square, which implies the presence of straight sides. Nevertheless, the sides of the square will not be detected by LSD because they are not edges. In this particular case it may be possible that a multiscale analysis is involved in our perception; and the sides are indeed detected by LSD at a different scale.

The resolution at which an image is analyzed is a very important factor. Figure 4.13 shows an example where a wrong scale analysis can lead to misinterpretations. The actual image has a resolution of $2,304 \times 3,072$ pixels. But at the scale printed on the page one can see neither the full resolution nor the individual pixels. Looking at the image as it appears printed, one would expect to detect the borders of the windows as line segments. LSD actually found many line segments per window. This can be explained by the presence of Venetian blinds, as shown in the details of the images shown in Fig. 4.13c,d. The detection is correct for the full resolution image. (Notice, however, that the vertical and diagonal black lines produce no detection, an effect similar to the one shown in Fig. 4.12.) To obtain a detection that corresponds to our perception of the printed image, the resolution of the image must be correctly reduced to keep the detail level that we are able to see. This procedure was followed in (*e*) which produces the expected result (*f*). A similar example is shown in Fig. 4.25.

A related problem appears with strongly quantized geometric pictures as shown in Fig. 4.14. The image is composed only of line segments, none of them detected by LSD. Strictly speaking, the pixels represent a "stair" pattern and not slanted line segments. See the details on the center of the figure. On the right, the level-line angles are represented by dashes. One can see the alternation between horizontal and 45 degree angles. This kind of "stair effect" is often generated by simple geometric drawing programs. A simple solution is obtained by a multiscale approach, as shown in the bottom images of the figure. The initial scaling step in LSD described in Sect. 3.3 is indeed doing that. The use of a bigger angle tolerance in the region growing algorithm could solve it too, but at the price of bad results in many other images.

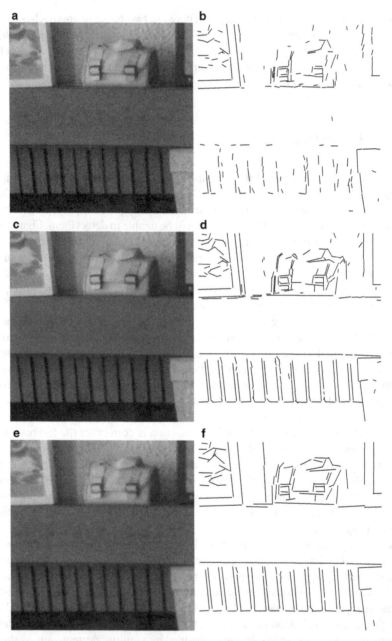

Fig. 4.11 (a) Part of a photo taken in low light conditions, 512×512 pixels. (b) Line segments detected by LSD. (c) The same image denoised using NL-means [12]. (d) Line segments detected after the NL-means step. (e) Analysis at a coarser scale: the image was filtered with a Gaussian filter of $\sigma = \sqrt{2}$ and then subsampled by a factor of 2. (f) Line segments obtained by LSD. (These experiments were done without the 80% image scaling described in Sect. 3.3; here we want to analyze how noise affects the region growing process, but the image filtering performed as part of the scaling would have helped the region growing algorithm)

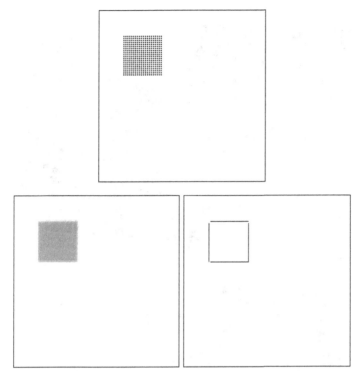

Fig. 4.12 The pattern of dots in the top figure will probably be perceived as a square. Nevertheless, the perceived sides of the square are not detected by LSD because they are not straight edges. Our perception probably uses a multiscale analysis. The bottom pair is the image and line segments found at a scale 8 times smaller

Another kind of problem is related to structured textures. Figure 4.15 illustrates the problem. On the background of the image there are some trees that produce the detection of some small line segments. A similar effect can be seen in the floor, due to the texture on the icy floor and the presence of shadows. A closer look (c) reveals that these detections correspond to locally straight structures really present in the image. From a low-level point of view they are not false detections. What makes this result strange is that it is not compatible with our semantic interpretation of the image. The only true solution for this problem will probably come from an analysis of the scene at a higher level.

As commented in the previous section, a multiscale approach can be used to handle noise. Figures 4.6, 4.17 and 4.18 show detections that cope with noise by analysis at different scales.

4.4 Comparison with Other Methods

This section compares the behavior of three *a contrario* line segment detectors to other popular methods. The comparison has no intention of being exhaustive as many algorithms are not considered; the experiments considered show typical

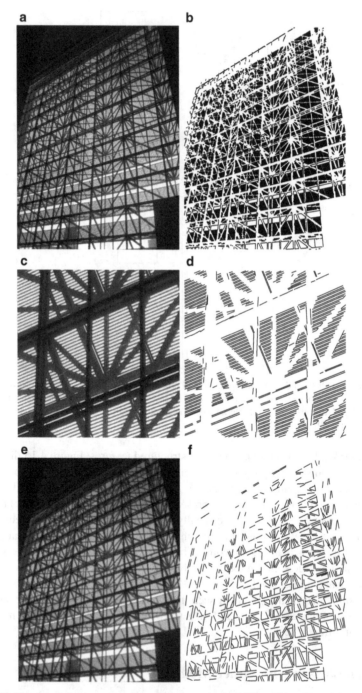

Fig. 4.13 This figure shows an apparent misinterpretation by LSD resulting from an inappropriate comparison. To make a fair comparison, the resolution of the image given to LSD must correspond to the scale at which one sees the image. (**a**) The original image, 2,304 × 3,072 pixels. At the size

results and the comments will focus on the relative strengths and weaknesses of the *a contrario* approach and will not attempt to describe the general behavior of line segment detectors.

The algorithms used are: the Hough transform method as implemented in the freely available package Xhoughtool [45]; Etemadi's algorithm in its original implementation in ORT-2.3; Burns et al.'s algorithm, using an implementation by Ross Beveridge [75] (personal communication); PPHT as implemented in the freely available RAVL-1.1.1 library; Desolneux et al.'s algorithm, as implemented in the module align_mdl included in the freely available image processing framework MegaWave2[1]; the multisegment detector in its original implementation; and finally LSD, freely available [36]. The aim of the *a contrario* approach is to develop automatic algorithms, which can be used without the need to tune parameters for each image. Accordingly, the experiments shown here were done without any parameter tuning on any of the algorithms presented; the default parameters for each one were used. Some of these algorithms can produce better results by selecting appropriate parameters; in some applications this is possible and convenient. As a result, the experiments presented here evaluate only one aspect of the algorithms: their performance as fully automatic analysis tools. The computation times are reported for each algorithm. The experiments were done on an Apple PowerBook G4 1.5 GHz, 1.25 GB of memory, and running Mac OS X 10.4.11.

The first experiment compares the line segment detections on a geometrical drawing, Fig. 4.16. One would expect good results for such a kind of image, but the results show that the image is actually challenging. Many of the algorithms give imprecise results, missing several detections. LSD is able to perform a correct detection at the original image scale. But some of the small line segments are just over the detection threshold, and when the 80% scaling described in Sect. 3.3 is applied they are no longer detectable because of their small size. This initial scaling improves the results in many cases at the price of missing some small line segments that could be otherwise detectable.

Figures 4.17 and 4.18 compare the results of these algorithms in the presence of noise. Among the *a contrario* algorithms, only LSD result is given as all of them produce similar results for these images: In stark contrast to other methods, the *a contrario* approach produces few detections when noise dominates the image. This is what we call the "threshold problem". Without a principled method to set thresholds, the number of detections explodes as noise is added.

Fig. 4.13 (continued) printed on this page it is not possible to see the individual pixels. This implies that what is perceived is a lower resolution version of the image. (**b**) Line segments found by LSD. Some zones seem black because there are many superposed line segments. The result, done at full resolution, differs from the expected one for the printed image. (**c**) A detail of the image can explain the result. (**d**) The Venetian blinds in the windows generate multiple parallel detections. The result is correct at the full resolution of the image. (**e**) To obtain the expected result the image must be correctly sub-sampled. (**f**) In the sub-sampled version LSD found the expected result

---

[1] http://megawave.cmla.ens-cachan.fr.

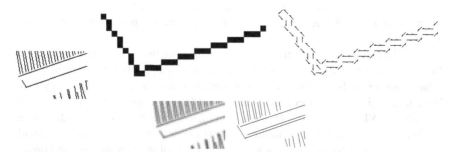

Fig. 4.14 *Top-Left:* an image representing strongly quantized line segments. LSD does not detect any of them. *Top-Center:* a detail of the image. One can see the stair effect of quantization. Strictly speaking, the image does not represent line segments. *Top-Right:* The dashes represent the level-line angles. As one can see, there is an alternation of horizontal and slanted dashes. *Bottom-Left:* Again, a multiscale approach can solve the problem, the same image at half scale. *Bottom-Right:* the line segments detected. Note that some of the line segments are too small to be detected. (These experiments were done without the 80% image scaling described in Sect. 3.3; the scaling step is added precisely to handle this problem)

Fig. 4.15 Structured textures can produce unexpected detections. (**a**) Original image. (**b**) Line segments found by LSD. (**c**) A detail of the image near the upper-right corner of the image. (**d**) The same detailed image with the detected line segments superposed. One can see that they correspond to structures present on the image. The solution for this conflict will probably come from a higher-level analysis of the scene

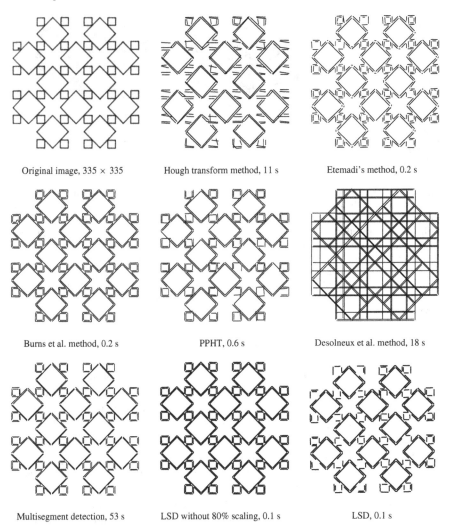

Original image, 335 × 335   Hough transform method, 11 s   Etemadi's method, 0.2 s

Burns et al. method, 0.2 s   PPHT, 0.6 s   Desolneux et al. method, 18 s

Multisegment detection, 53 s   LSD without 80% scaling, 0.1 s   LSD, 0.1 s

Fig. 4.16 A comparison between various line segment detection methods. Etemadi's method detects line segments and arcs at the same time; here only the line segments are shown. On this simple geometric image one would expect good results with any line segment detection method. This is not the case. The Hough transform method fails to detect many of the line segments of the image, and gives imprecise results for the detected ones. Etemadi's method does a better job, but still there are missing line segments and imprecise ones. The Burns et al. algorithm gives a good result (but gives some small line segments caused by the threshold problem). PPHT detects almost all the expected line segments, but the result is not very precise. Desolneux et al. misinterprets the information giving long line segments. The multisegment detector and LSD without the 80% scaling described in Sect. 3.3 give the (intuitively) correct result. The multisegment detector is also able to capture the global alignment of the small line segments. Some line segments are missed by LSD when the 80% scaling described in Sect. 3.3 is applied; the reason is that their lengths are just over the detection limit and get under the detection threshold after the 80% scaling

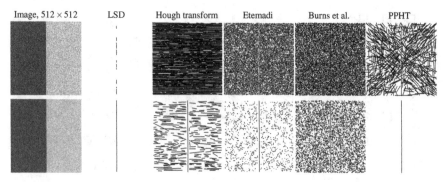

Fig. 4.17 Analysis of a noisy edge image at two different scales by five line segment detection algorithms. When the noise is important (here Gaussian noise with $\sigma = 50$), LSD will not detect some of the line segments that we can see; it will not produce false detections either. The methods without a false detection control produce many false detections, rendering the result useless. PPHT false detection control failed in this case. PPHT and Etemadi's method did, indeed, detect the edge (along with numerous false positives) at full resolution; this is because the detection relies on Canny edge points, which involves a Gaussian filtering. A standard way to cope with noise is by Gaussian subsampling. LSD and PPHT, both produce the expected result at half resolution (second row); the Hough transform method, Etemadi's method, and the Burns et al. method still produce false detections

As explained in Sect. 1.4, the PPHT algorithm includes a false detection control mechanism which significantly reduces the threshold problem. Nevertheless, this mechanism is not completely satisfactory as it is based on controlling the *probability* that a candidate produces a false detection. As the image size is increased, the number of line segments tested is extremely large and, even with a small probability of detection, many false detections are produced as Figs. 4.17 and 4.18 show. Also, the false detection method can miss some short line segments while producing longer false detections, as shown in Fig. 1.3.

As described in Sect. 4.2, analyzing the image at a reduced scale allows the *a contrario* methods to detect the structures masked by noise at full scale. Figures 4.17 and 4.18 illustrate this, showing the results for the same images at half scale in the former case and half and 1/4 scale in the latter. The true structure is detected by all the methods at reduced scales. However, the other methods report also a high number of false positives.

The *a contrario* algorithms were designed to prevent detections in noise. But the non-accidentalness criterion prevents other kind of accidental detections too. Even if there is no significant noise in the image of Fig. 4.20, the methods without an *a contrario* validation produce false detections due to the rough texture of the keys. A similar example is shown in Fig. 4.21, caused in this case by the texture of vegetation. The *a contrario* methods do produce some false detections of this kind, as explained in the last section and illustrated in Fig. 4.15, but the magnitude of the problem is considerably reduced.

This threshold problem in textured zones is actually very common and it is observed to some degree in the results on most natural images, see Figs. 4.22 and 4.23. The threshold problem is clear in the Hough transform method, Etemadi's

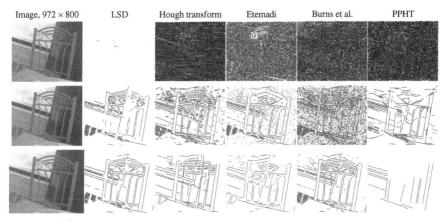

Image, 972 × 800   LSD   Hough transform   Etemadi   Burns et al.   PPHT

Fig. 4.18 The same effect shown in Fig. 4.17 can be seen on a noisy natural image. The input image is the one in the first row of Fig. 4.10 with added Gaussian noise ($\sigma = 30$). The three rows correspond to the analysis at full scale, 1/2 resolution and 1/4 resolution by Gaussian sub-sampling. At full resolution, LSD fails to detect the structure of the image, but produces no false detection. Algorithms without a false detection control, like the Hough transform method, Etemadi's method, and Burns et al.'s method, produce not usable results. PPHT false detection control fails in this image and produces many false detections. The structure of the image cannot be obtained at full resolution when noise dominates. But the image can be analyzed at a different scale (like human vision probably does). Most of the structure is detected by LSD at half resolution. Note that the PPHT method and Etemadi's method detect part of the structure of the image at full resolution; the reason is that both approaches use Canny points, which involves a Gaussian filtering

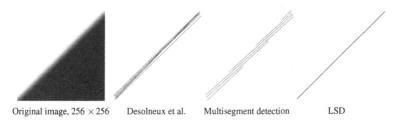

Original image, 256 × 256   Desolneux et al.   Multisegment detection   LSD

Fig. 4.19 Blurred edges may lead the Desolneux et al. method and the multisegment detector to produce parallel line segments arising from the same image edge

algorithm, and Burns et al.'s algorithm, resulting in a huge quantity of tiny line segments. A decision rule is needed to select line segments; otherwise, the detection is useless. For many applications, of course, manual parameter tuning is acceptable and these methods can be successfully used.

Hough transform method and the PPHT algorithm do not use gradient angle information nor edge points chaining. As a result, unrelated points may be grouped into complete false detections with orientations unrelated to image edges, see Figs. 4.17, 4.18, 4.20, and 4.21. The gradient information could also be used to improve the lack of accuracy of valid detections, especially short ones. Improved versions of these algorithms incorporate the gradient angle information [28].

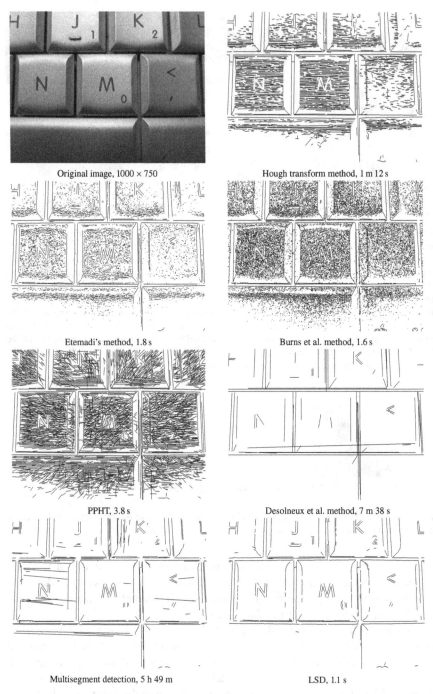

Original image, 1000 × 750

Hough transform method, 1 m 12 s

Etemadi's method, 1.8 s

Burns et al. method, 1.6 s

PPHT, 3.8 s

Desolneux et al. method, 7 m 38 s

Multisegment detection, 5 h 49 m

LSD, 1.1 s

Fig. 4.20 Keyboard: There is no significant noise in this image; the texture on the keys leads, however, some algorithms to produce many false detections. (This experiment is a tribute to my trusty Apple PowerBook G4 12-inch where most of this work was done. This book is going to be its last mission)

Original image, 1024×768

Hough transform method, 2 m 41 s

Etemadi's method, 8 s

Burns et al. method, 2.2 s

PPHT, 5.8 s

Desolneux et al. method, 6 m 52 s

Multisegment detection, 10 h 44 m

LSD, 1.6 s

Fig. 4.21 Hasselö: The texture of vegetation is in many aspects similar to noise. Nevertheless, it is not completely isotropic; the tendency to global structures of Desolneux et al. method and the multisegment detector produce long false detections

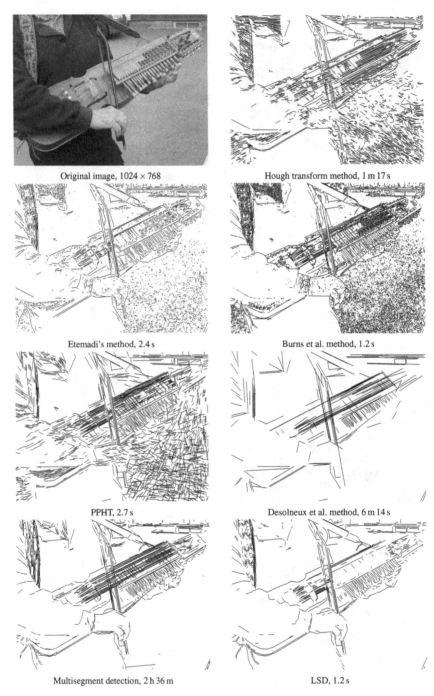

Original image, 1024 × 768

Hough transform method, 1 m 17 s

Etemadi's method, 2.4 s

Burns et al. method, 1.2 s

PPHT, 2.7 s

Desolneux et al. method, 6 m 14 s

Multisegment detection, 2 h 36 m

LSD, 1.2 s

Fig. 4.22 Nyckelharpa: The background texture leads to false detections in some algorithms. The tendency to global structures of Desolneux et al. method and the multisegment detector produces correct detection of the strings of the musical instrument

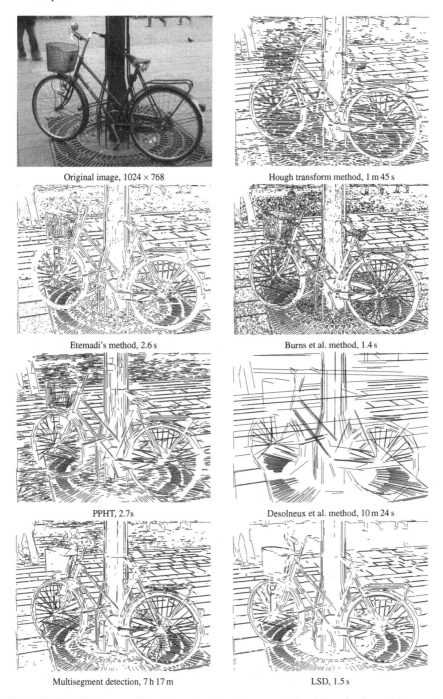

Original image, 1024 × 768

Hough transform method, 1 m 45 s

Etemadi's method, 2.6 s

Burns et al. method, 1.4 s

PPHT, 2.7 s

Desolneux et al. method, 10 m 24 s

Multisegment detection, 7 h 17 m

LSD, 1.5 s

Fig. 4.23 Bike: Being a non linear-time algorithm, the computational time for the multisegment detector grows very fast with the image size. It requires several hours of computations to produce this result; this image size approaches the practical limit of this method

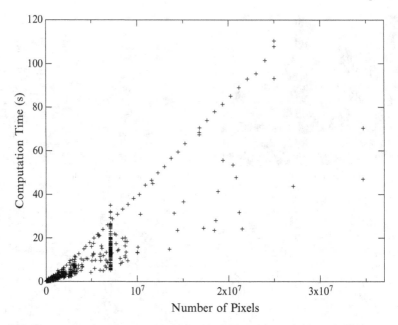

Fig. 4.24 Computation time (in seconds) required by LSD for the processing of 1297 images as a function of the image size (total number of pixels). The computations were done with LSD running on an Apple PowerBook G4 1.5 GHz. The slanted linear series corresponds to Gaussian white noise images. The vertical linear series corresponds to images of size 3,072 × 2,304, a common camera resolution when the experiment was done

Desolneux et al. method produces few false detections, but fails to get the right interpretation when aligned line segments are present. The misinterpretations result in most cases in the production of long line segments encompassing shorter and aligned ones, as in Figs. 1.3, 2.16, 4.16, 4.20 and 4.23. In some cases, the algorithm groups together line segments that are not well aligned, producing imprecise results. The multisegment detector makes the same mistake.

A problem which is shared by Desolneux et al. method and by the multisegment detector is the handling of wide line segments; in this situation both algorithms produce many parallel detections, see the Fig. 4.19.

Desolneux et al. method and the multisegment detector also share a bias towards global aligned structures. This can be clearly seen in Fig. 2.16. The Desolneux et al. method produces long line segments where two smaller ones are well aligned. The multisegment detector prefers interpretations where line segments of two or three combs are aligned; when the edges are not well aligned, it leads to fragmentation and slanted line segments. The bias towards long aligned structures make that some line segments detected on texture are joined into long false detections instead of short ones, see the grass in Fig. 4.21. Inversely, this same tendency to global alignments leads to the correct detection of the tiling in Fig. 4.21 and the strings of the musical instrument in Fig. 4.22.

Fig. 4.25 One of the images that gives the longer processing time per pixel by LSD. It takes 35 s for 3,072 × 2,304 pixels, or about 5 μs per pixel on an Apple PowerBook G4 1.5 GHz. The mix of a large quantity of small size grass structures and the background "noise" of the even smaller grass structures, gives the worst computational case. As in Fig. 4.13, the image cannot be seen in full resolution in this page. The second row shows a detail of the image in full resolution to illustrate the fact that the small line segments are justified. A correct analysis of this image probably involves a multiscale analysis as discussed in Sect. 4.2

4.5 Computational Time

This section presents an empirical study of the computational efficiency of the LSD algorithm. Figure 4.24 shows a plot of the computational time in seconds versus the image size, when using an Apple PowerBook G4 1.5 GHz. The computational time is roughly linear with the number of pixels in the image, which corresponds to a linear-time algorithm. For most images the computation time is shorter than for a white noise image of the same size (the slanted linear series of points on the plot). The main reason is that, in natural images, many pixels are discarded by the gradient threshold. Some images, however, require longer processing time than white noise images, as can be seen on the plot. It is usually the case in images with noise-like structures and long-range structures on the foreground. Figure 4.25 shows an example. The mix of thousands of small size grass structures (where rectangular approximation and NFA computations are done) and the background "noise" of even smaller grass structures (that keeps LSD searching for line-support regions) gives the worst computational time.

Chapter 5
Extensions

No existing algorithm for line segment detection can be said to perform this task to full satisfaction. The problem is indeed ill-posed: people often disagree about the exact set of line segments that corresponds to a particular image, revealing differences in the basic notion or in the interpretation of a given scene. But current algorithms are still far from this level of disagreement, producing failures universally recognized as such. As a simple example, none of the full scale results in Fig. 4.17 is satisfactory. These failures essentially show that the definitions of line segment implicitly used are not good enough.

Each family of failures points to a shortcoming of the LSD algorithm and each one suggests improvements to the methods. The previous chapter commented on some of the limitations of the *a contrario* method. Section 4.3 explained the need for a multiscale approach. Integrating the information at different scales is a necessary, but very challenging problem. This chapter will comment on the principal extensions needed, illustrating the difficulties and giving some hints to possible solutions.

5.1 Contrast and Edge Definition

We are discussing the problem of line segment detection or locally straight edge detection. A fundamental problem is then how to define *edges*. Informally, edges are highly-contrasted zones or sharp transitions of image brightness. It is not trivial, however, to give a precise meaning to "high contrast" that is useful and well founded at the same time.

In LSD, the *a contrario* method is applied to the level-line angular structure of the zone to be evaluated. A region that is significantly anisotropic usually corresponds to a locally straight edge. But not always. Common counterexamples are slow gradients due to illumination changes. This is often observed in the sky or on uniform walls. To prevent detections on this kind of zones, the methods described here use a simple and classic approach for handling contrast: a pixel is considered as highly contrasted when the modulus of the image gradient exceeds a threshold, see

R. Grompone von Gioi, *A Contrario Line Segment Detection*, SpringerBriefs in Computer Science, DOI 10.1007/978-1-4939-0575-1_5, © The Author(s) 2014

Fig. 5.1 A fixed threshold on the image gradient magnitude does not provide an appropriate edge definition. *Left*: A subtle but visible edge from gray-levels 125 to 130 (exaggerated here for print). *Right*: A soft gradient, 50 pixels wide, from gray-levels 3 to 248. Any threshold that detects the edge in the left hand image would also detect edges at every point in the right hand image

Sect. 3.6. This method, however, is not satisfactory as it is illustrated in Fig. 5.1. An image step of a few gray levels can be visible if the transition is sharp. The same image gradient modulus can be observed in a smooth transition of an image or even under noise conditions. The gradient threshold in LSD is selected in order to reject pixels where the gradient angle has a large error due to quantization noise. The criterion is designed to cope with the worst quantization case and for the same reason, it may miss some low contrasted edges.

A second problem is related to the width of the edge. The LSD algorithm groups together connected pixels that share roughly the same gradient orientation. But this is not always the right thing to do. The image in Fig. 5.2 shows two edges separated by a gray zone. But actually, the gray zone is a slow transition from dark gray at left to a brighter gray at right (see the brightness profile in the center of the figure). As a result, the image gradient has the same orientation in the central gray zone as in the edges (right). (Also, the image gradient magnitude is large enough to overcome the threshold.) Thus, LSD groups together the gray zone and the two edges into *one* region, producing only one wide line segment.

There is an extensive literature on the problem of edge detection [66], discussing these kinds of problems. The natural answer in our context is to use the *a contrario* framework in handling image brightness and contrast. As a simple assumption, the non-structured model can be set to Gaussian white noise of known power. Then, edges would be detected as outliers to that model by thresholds that control the expected number of false detections on it. This kind of approach was proposed several times in the literature [1, 6, 24, 29], not necessarily labeled as an *a contrario* framework, but the same core ideas are used. For the method to work fully automatic, a noise power estimation algorithm must also be integrated [53]. The effective integration of all these steps is, however, far from being a trivial task.

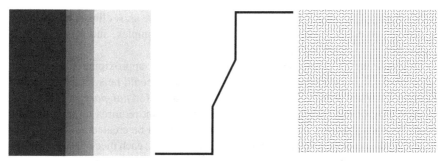

Fig. 5.2 A particularly tricky image for the LSD algorithm (*left*). The perceptual impression is of two edges separated by a gray zone. Actually, the central gray zone has a soft gradient, as the brightness profile shows (*center*). The two edges and the gray zone share the same level-line orientations (*right*). As result, the region growing algorithm will produce only one line-support region covering the two edges and the gray zone. Contrary to our perception, LSD will detect one wide line segment instead of two. (The level-line element arrowheads were not drawn here)

5.2 Curves

Human made objects often contain flat surfaces and straight edges. For this reason, pictures of human environments usually accept an economic description in terms of line segments. Nevertheless, a large part of the edges are not really straight, but curved. In such cases, the algorithms described here produce an approximation to these edges, see for example, Fig. 4.2. Algorithms especially designed for handling curves can significantly improve the results.

When LSD is used to approximate a curved edge, the result is a list of line segments without any information about their relative position; for example, nothing in the result indicates that two line segments are consecutive along the same edge. A first improvement is then to chain line segments, transforming a list of isolated elements into approximated curves. A simple way is to chain the already found line segments by evaluating local properties between their end points. (A simple, but unsatisfactory algorithm of this kind is described in [32].) A better approach is to include the chaining operation into the heuristic that selects candidates: when a line segment is found, the next seed pixel is selected near its end points; this way the chaining is done naturally as the detector follows the curve.

Chaining the elements as they are found also allows for a finer control of how curves are approximated by line segments. New problems are introduced by the same token; for example, how to handle edge bifurcations or how to choose the best point to cut the curve into elements. This is related to the classic problem of polygonal approximation of curves [69, 71, 76, 84]. Some of these algorithms require the full curve to be known in advance; the heuristic search could start from the full set of chained edge pixels and the resulting polygonal approximation would provide the line segment candidates. The approximation of curves implies a compromise between accurate and economic descriptions. A natural way to improve both aspects is to include richer families of curve elements, like circle arcs, ellipse arcs, splines or Bézier curves [74]. The topology of 2D curves is complex, and it is a difficult task to design a general and efficient method.

In classic approaches, the decision about the best approximation is usually based on fixed geometric thresholds. These thresholds could be selected using the *a contrario* framework. Such an *a contrario* method for *flat parts* of curves is described by Cao et al. [15, ch.3]; this approach, again, requires to have the full curve before processing. A simple online algorithm can be created to extend LSD by adding *a contrario* validation for other curve elements; each piece of curve would be evaluated and the best interpretation in NFA terms would be kept.

The ELSD algorithm by Pătrăucean et al. [67, 68] is a first attempt to extend LSD for handling curves. It uses line segments, circular arcs and elliptical arcs as curve elements. The formulation of the *a contrario* framework is very similar to the one for line segments described in Chap. 2. For each curve element, a pixel is said to be *aligned* when its level-line is tangent to the curve up to a certain tolerance. Figure 5.3 shows a circular arc with perfectly aligned pixels inside. Using the same *a contrario* model H_0, the number of aligned pixels follows a binomial distribution. An important difference is in the number of tests: each family—line segments, circle arcs, ellipse arcs—has a different size. For example, the number of circle arcs is roughly determined by the number of possible centers (NM in an $N \times M$ image), the number of possible radius values (about $\sqrt{NM}$), the number of possible initial and final arc angles (about $\sqrt{NM}$ for each), and the number of possible widths (also about $\sqrt{NM}$). The number of tests for the circle arcs family is about $(NM)^3$ and its NFA is

$$\text{NFA}_{\text{circ}} = (NM)^3 \cdot B(n, k, p) \, ,$$

where n is the total number of pixels in the arc ring, k is the number among them that is aligned to the arc, and p is the probability that pixels are aligned by chance in the *a contrario* model H_0. Similarly, the number of tests for full circles is $(NM)^2$, the family of full ellipses has a size of $(NM)^3$, and the family of elliptical arcs is about $(NM)^4$ [67, 68].

Figure 5.4 compares the results of LSD and ELSD on a synthetic image. Each piece of curve is evaluated as a line segment, circle, ellipse, etc. A small enough structure may only be accepted with the right primitive—for example, the central circle in Fig. 5.4. But most structures would produce detections of various kinds; the algorithm will choose the one with the smallest NFA value as the best interpretation. A richer family, as elliptical arcs, may lead to better approximation with a small probability term, reducing the NFA value; on the other hand, a larger family has a larger number of tests, increasing the NFA value. This conflict usually resolves into the right interpretation, as is the case in Fig. 5.4. The use of a continuous formulation as in Sect. 2.5 should allow to improve this selection step even more.

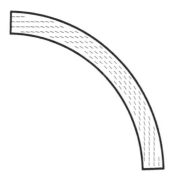

Fig. 5.3 *Left*: a circular arc ring and the level-line orientation field inside it. In this case all of them are perfectly *aligned pixels*. (The level-line element arrowheads were not drawn here)

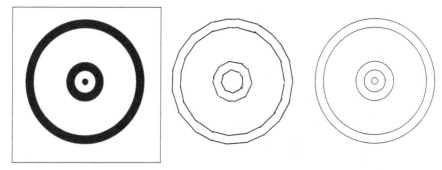

Fig. 5.4 *Left*: a synthetic image, 249×249 pixels. *Center*: the line segments detected by the LSD algorithm. *Right*: the circle arcs detected by the ELSD algorithm [68]. The small circle in the center produces no line segment detection. The larger circles, however, produce both line segment and circle detections. Selecting the interpretation with the smallest NFA value led in this case to the right interpretation

5.3 Multiscale Analysis

Section 4.3 showed that the scale of analysis is a very important factor for a line segment detector. Human vision is indeed able to correctly interpret many images where LSD fails, arguably by processing the retinal information at different scales at the same time. The same idea could be implemented in our algorithms.

After a quick look, Fig. 5.5 would probably be described as depicting some sort of triangular object. Thus, one could expect LSD to spot the three sides of the triangle as line segments. However, because of the "teeth" of the object, the sides are not detected by LSD. Actually, one of the sides has large enough teeth to produce detections themselves. Some kind of grouping of those small line segments could lead to the detection of the straight structure. But these sides can also be directly found at coarser scale, as is shown in the figure. The results obtained at different scales are redundant for some structures, complementary for others, and inconsistent for still others. A fundamental and challenging problem is how to combine these detections, reducing redundancy and solving conflicts.

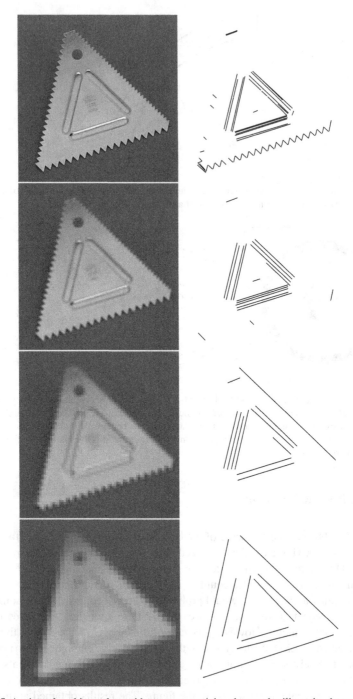

Fig. 5.5 A triangular object whose sides are not straight edges and will not be detected at full scale. On the right are shown the line segments found by LSD. The different rows show the result of a multiscale analysis by sub-sampling

There have been many attempts to provide multiscale analysis of images. Some of these methods, like wavelets analysis [57, 58], handle each scale independently without merging or solving conflicts. Several methods were proposed to merge data from different scales; the scale-space method being a good example [50, 86]. Other proposals include explicit criteria to select the appropriate scale [24, 54]. An effective incorporation of these ideas would lead to a multiscale version of LSD.

Nevertheless, the complexity of the problem should not be underestimated. Human visual environments are extremely rich, but only part of the information is relevant and is distributed at different scales. The example in Fig. 5.5 is very simple, but still, an automatic analysis that integrates the different scales is unknown. The human visual system probably solves the problem by finding a global interpretation for the whole data; Gestalt theory would imply this kind of approach. This is indeed a central problem in visual perception and it is not expected to be a satisfactory solution based on simple tricks. Current algorithms work well when they act at a low level of interpretation, without exploiting or destroying high-level information. All we can hope for the time being is to correctly merge information at different scales to produce an accurate *geometrical* description of the image structure.

5.4 Color and Video

The algorithms described here were all designed to handle individual grayscale images. They can be applied to color images or videos by converting them to grayscale and processing videos frame by frame. This will produce useful results in the general case; some examples are available at the IPOL article about the LSD algorithm [36]. This approach, however, disregards an important part of the information available, which leads to missing or inaccurate detections.

Color images are usually composed of three channels, providing the intensity for each of the three color components at each pixel. In other words, pixel values in color images are vectors instead of scalars, as in grayscale images. When a color image is converted to grayscale, the intensity of each pixel is computed as the weighted mean of the intensity of its channels. Two very different colors may have the same mean intensity and would be converted to the same gray value. One can easily build an image whose left half side is green and the right half side is red, but when converted to grayscale, it results in an uniform gray image [36]. Even if there is a clearly visible edge in the color image, a line segment detector or edge detector that operates on the grayscale image will fail to detect it.

This is a well-known problem that led to the creation of a particular field of color image edge detection [64]. Roughly speaking, there are two strategies: to process each image component separately and then combine the result; or to use an operator that takes vector values and gives a measure of its difference in a similar way that the gradient does for scalar values. Both strategies can be applied to produce an line segment detector that handles color images directly.

The first approach would apply the line segment detector to each color channel (or to each component of a different color space), merging afterward the resulting line segments. However, merging the results may reveal a difficult task: the same edge may produce partial line segments at each channel, and their combination is far from trivial, especially when the accuracy of the detections is low. This merging problem shares some of the difficulties of the multiscale merging problem described in Sect. 5.3.

The second strategy provides, at first view, a straightforward extension of our methods to color images. Nevertheless, not all the operators proposed for color edge detection are appropriate for a direct extension of LSD: in addition to a measure of the intensity of the edge, a suitable operator must also provide the edge orientation. More importantly, in order to ground the validation method on a solid base, one should be able to justify the isotropic and independent *a contrario* model for the level-line field, or alternatively provide a more suitable one.

Similar considerations can be made about line segment detection in video. Videos have strong temporal redundancy and significant information is ignored by a frame by frame processing. The same two strategies are possible here. Line segments could be first computed on each frame individually, improving the accuracy later by matching the results of consecutive frames. Alternatively, line segment detection could operate on a level-line field computed by an edge operator acting on three or more consecutive frames. As for color, neither of the strategies provides a straightforward solution.

References

1. Abraham, I., Abraham, R., Desolneux, A., Li-Thiao-Te, S.: Significant edges in the case of non-stationary Gaussian noise. Pattern Recognition **40**, 3277–3291 (2007)
2. Agrawal, M., Kayal, N., Saxena, N.: PRIMES is in P. Annals of Mathematics **160**(2), 781–793 (2004)
3. Albert, M.K., Hoffman, D.D.: Genericity in spatial vision. In: D. Luce, K. Romney, D. Hoffman, D'Zmura M. (eds.) Geometric Representations of Perceptual Phenomena: Articles in Honor of Tarow Indow's 70th Birthday, pp. 95–112.— Erlbaum (1995)
4. Almansa, A.: Echantillonnage, interpolation et détection. Applications en imagerie satellitaire. Ph.D. thesis, ENS Cachan (2002)
5. Almansa, A., Desolneux, A., Vamech, S.: Vanishing point detection without any a priori information. IEEE Transactions on Pattern Analysis and Machine Intelligence **25**(4), 502–507 (2003)
6. Alpert, S., Galun, M., Nadler, B., Basri, R.: Detecting faint curved edges in noisy images. In: K. Daniilidis, P. Maragos, N. Paragios (eds.) Computer Vision – ECCV 2010, *Lecture Notes in Computer Science*, vol. 6314, pp. 750–763. Springer Berlin/Heidelberg (2010)
7. Arp, H., Hazard, C.: Peculiar configurations of quasars in two adjacent areas of the sky. The Astrophysical Journal **240**(3), 726–736 (1980)
8. Attneave, F.: Informational aspects of visual perception. Psychological Review **61**, 183–193 (1954)
9. Ballard, D.H.: Generalizing the Hough transform to detect arbitrary shapes. Pattern recognition **13**(2), 111–122 (1981)
10. Binford, T.O.: Inferring surfaces from images. Artificial Intelligence **17**, 205–244 (1981)
11. Borwein, J.M., Borwein, P.B., Bailey, D.H.: Ramanujan, modular equations, and approximations to Pi or how to compute one billion digits of Pi. The American Mathematical Monthly **96**(3), 201–219 (1989)
12. Buades, A., Coll, B., Morel, J.M.: A non-local algorithm for image denoising. In: Computer Vision and Pattern Recognition, 2005. CVPR 2005. IEEE Computer Society Conference on, vol. 2, pp. 60–65 (2005)
13. Burns, J.B., Hanson, A.R., Riseman, E.M.: Extracting straight lines. IEEE Transactions on Pattern Analysis and Machine Intelligence **8**(4), 425–455 (1986)
14. Canny, J.: A computational approach to edge detection. IEEE Transactions on Pattern Analysis and Machine Intelligence **8**(6), 679–698 (1986)
15. Cao, F., Lisani, J.L., Morel, J.M., Musé, P., Sur, F.: A Theory of Shape Identification. Springer (2008)
16. Christensen, R.: Testing Fisher, Neyman, Pearson, and Bayes. The American Statistician **59**(2), 121–126 (2005)
17. Copeland, B.J. (ed.): The Essential Turing. Clarendon Press (2004)

R. Grompone von Gioi, *A Contrario Line Segment Detection*, SpringerBriefs in Computer Science, DOI 10.1007/978-1-4939-0575-1, © The Author(s) 2014

18. Dembski, W.A.: The Design Inference: Eliminating chance through small probabilities. Cambridge University Press (1998)
19. Desolneux, A., Moisan, L., Morel, J.M.: Meaningful alignments. International Journal of Computer Vision **40**(1), 7–23 (2000)
20. Desolneux, A., Moisan, L., Morel, J.M.: Maximal meaningful events and applications to image analysis. The Annals of Statistics **31**(6), 1822–1851 (2003)
21. Desolneux, A., Moisan, L., Morel, J.M.: Gestalt theory and computer vision. In: A. Carsetti (ed.) Seeing, Thinking and Knowing: Meaning and Self-Organization in Visual Cognition and Thought, pp. 71–101. Kluwer Academic Publishers (2004)
22. Desolneux, A., Moisan, L., Morel, J.M.: From Gestalt Theory to Image Analysis, a Probabilistic Approach. Springer (2008)
23. Edmunds, M.G., H., G.G.: Random alignment of quasars. Nature **290**, 481–483 (1981)
24. Elder, J.H., Zucker, S.W.: Local scale control for edge detection and blur estimation. IEEE Transactions on Pattern Analysis and Machine Intelligence **20**(7), 699–716 (1998)
25. Etemadi, A.: Robust segmentation of edge data. International Conference on Image Processing and its Applications pp. 311–314 (1992)
26. Faugeras, O., Deriche, R., Mathieu, H., Ayache, N.J., Randall, G.: The depth and motion analysis machine. International Journal of Pattern Recognition and Artificial Intelligence **6**(2–3), 353–385 (1992)
27. Fisher, R.A.: Statistical Methods and Scientific Inference, second edn. Oliver and Boyd (1959)
28. Galambos, C., Kittler, J., Matas, J.: Gradient based progressive probabilistic Hough transform. Vision, Image and Signal Processing, IEE Proceedings – **148**(3), 158–165 (2001)
29. Galun, M., Basri, R., Brandt, A.: Multiscale edge detection and fiber enhancement using differences of oriented means. IEEE 11th International Conference on Computer Vision (ICCV 2007) pp. 1–8 (2007)
30. Grompone von Gioi, R.: Toward a computational theory of perception. In: Proceedings of the Fifth Asia-Pacific Computing and Philosophy Conference. Tokyo, Japan (2009)
31. Grompone von Gioi, R.: Inverse geometry: Graphical interpretation of images. Ph.D. thesis, ENS Cachan, France (2010)
32. Grompone von Gioi, R., Delon, J., Morel, J.M.: The collaboration of grouping laws in vision. Journal of Physiology – Paris **106**(5–6), 266–283 (2012)
33. Grompone von Gioi, R., Jakubowicz, J.: On computational Gestalt detection thresholds. Journal of Physiology – Paris **103**(1–2), 4–17 (2009)
34. Grompone von Gioi, R., Jakubowicz, J., Morel, J.M., Randall, G.: On straight line segment detection. Journal of Mathematical Imaging and Vision **32**(3), 313–347 (2008)
35. Grompone von Gioi, R., Jakubowicz, J., Morel, J.M., Randall, G.: LSD: A fast Line Segment Detector with a false detection control. IEEE Transactions on Pattern Analysis and Machine Intelligence **32**(4), 722–732 (2010)
36. Grompone von Gioi, R., Jakubowicz, J., Morel, J.M., Randall, G.: LSD: a Line Segment Detector. Image Processing On Line (2012). URL http://dx.doi.org/10.5201/ipol.2012.gjmr-lsd
37. Grompone von Gioi, R., Jakubowicz, J., Randall, G.: Multisegment detection. IEEE International Conference on Image Processing **2**, 253–256 (2007)
38. Gordon, A., Glazko, G., Qiu, X., Yakovlev, A.: Control of the mean number of false discoveries, Bonferroni and stability of multiple testing. The Annals of Applied Statistics **1**(1), 179–190 (2007)
39. Hochberg, Y., Tamhane, A.C.: Multiple comparison procedures. John Wiley & Sons, New York (1987)
40. Hough, P.V.C.: Method and Means for Recognizing Complex Patterns. U.S. Patent 3,069,654 (Dec. 18, 1962)
41. Hubbard, R., Bayarri, M.J.: Confusion over measures of evidence (p's) versus errors (α's) in classical statistical testing. The American Statistician **57**(3), 171–178 (2003)
42. Igual, L., Preciozzi, J., Garrido, L., Almansa, A., Caselles, V., Rougé, B.: Automatic low baseline stereo in urban areas. Inverse Problems and Imaging **1**(2), 319–348 (2007)

43. Kahn, P., Kitchen, L., Riseman, E.M.: Real-time feature extraction: A fast line finder for vision-guided robot navigation. Tech. Rep. 87–57, University of Massachusetts, Computer and Information Science (1987)

44. Kahn, P., Kitchen, L., Riseman, E.M.: A fast line finder for vision-guided robot navigation. IEEE Transactions on Pattern Analysis and Machine Intelligence **12**(11), 1098–1102 (1990)

45. Kälviäinen, H., Hirvonen, P., Oja, E.: Houghtool — a software package for the use of the Hough transform. Pattern Recognition Letters **17**(8), 889–897 (1996)

46. Kanizsa, G.: Grammatica del vedere. Società editrice il Mulino (1980)

47. Klette, R., Rosenfeld, A.: Digital straightness—a review. Discrete Applied Mathematics **139**, 197–230 (2004)

48. Knuth, D.E.: The Art of Computer Programming, vol. 1: Fundamental Algorithms, third edn. Addison-Wesley (1997)

49. Knuth, D.E.: The Art of Computer Programming, vol. 2: Seminumerical Algorithms, third edn. Addison-Wesley (1998)

50. Koenderink, J.J.: The structure of images. Biological cybernetics **50**(5), 363–370 (1984)

51. Köhler, W.: Gestalt Psychology. Liveright (1947)

52. Koplowitz, J., Lindenbaum, M., Bruckstein, A.: The number of digital straight lines on an $N \times N$ grid. IEEE Transactions on Information Theory **36**(1), 192–197 (1990)

53. Lebrun, M., Colom, M., Buades, A., Morel, J.M.: Secrets of image denoising cuisine. Acta Numerica pp. 475–576 (2012)

54. Lindeberg, T.: Feature detection with automatic scale selection. International Journal of Computer Vision **20**(2), 79–116 (1998)

55. Lowe, D.: Perceptual Organization and Visual Recognition. Kluwer Academic Publishers (1985)

56. Lowe, D., Binford, T.O.: The interpretation of three-dimensional structure from image curves. Proceedings of IJCAI-7 pp. 613–618 (1981)

57. Mallat, S.G.: A theory for multiresolution signal decomposition: the wavelet representation. IEEE Transactions on Pattern Analysis and Machine Intelligence **11**(7), 674–693 (1989)

58. Mallat, S.G.: A wavelet tour of signal processing, second edn. Academic Press (1999)

59. Marichal, J.L., Mossinghoff, M.J.: Slices, slabs, and sections of the unit hypercube. Online Journal of Analytic Combinatorics **3** (2008)

60. Matas, J., Galambos, C., Kittler, J.: Robust detection of lines using the progressive probabilistic Hough transform. Computer Vision and Image Understanding **78**(1), 119–137 (2000)

61. Metzger, W.: Gesetze des Sehens, third edn. Verlag Waldemar Kramer, Frankfurt am Main (1975)

62. Metzger, W.: Laws of Seeing. The MIT Press (2006 (originally 1936)). English translation of the first edition of [61].

63. Minsky, M.: Computation: Finite and Infinite Machines. Prentice-Hall (1967)

64. Mittal, A., Sofat, S., Hancock, E.: Detection of edges in color images: A review and evaluative comparison of state-of-the-art techniques. In: M. Kamel, F. Karray, H. Hagras (eds.) Autonomous and Intelligent Systems, *Lecture Notes in Computer Science*, vol. 7326, pp. 250–259. Springer Berlin / Heidelberg (2012)

65. Newell, A., Simon, H.A.: Computer science as empirical inquiry: Symbols and search. Communications of the ACM **19**(3), 113–126 (1976)

66. Papari, G., Petkov, N.: Edge and line oriented contour detection: State of the art. Image and Vision Computing **29**, 79–103 (2011)

67. Pătrăucean, V.: Detection and identification of elliptical structure arrangements in images: theory and algorithms. Ph.D. thesis, IRIT, Toulouse, France (2012)

68. Pătrăucean, V., Gurdjos, P., Grompone von Gioi, R.: A parameterless line segment and elliptical arc detector with enhanced ellipse fitting. In: Computer Vision – ECCV 2012, pp. 572–585 (2012)

69. Perez, J.C., Vidal, E.: Optimum polygonal approximation of digitized curves. Pattern Recognition Letters **15**, 743–750 (1994)

70. Pomerantz, J.R., Kubovy, M.: Theoretical approaches to perceptual organization. In: K. Booff, L. Kaufmann, J. Thomas (eds.) Handbook of Perception and Human Performance: Vol. II. Cognitive Processes and Performance, pp. 36.1–36.46. Wiley, New York (1986)

71. Ramer, U.: An iterative procedure for the polygonal approximation of planar curves. Computer Graphics and Image Processing **1**, 244–256 (1972)

72. Rock, I.: The Logic of Perception. The MIT Press (1983)

73. Rosenfeld, A.: Digital straight line segments. TC **23**(12), 1264–1269 (1974)

74. Rosin, P.L., West, G.A.W.: Nonparametric segmentation of curves into various representations. IEEE Transactions on Pattern Analysis and Machine Intelligence **17**(12), 1140–1153 (1995)

75. Ross Beveridge, J., Graves, C., Lesher, C.: Some lessons learned from coding the Burns line extraction algorithm in the DARPA image understanding environment. Tech. Rep. CS-96–125, Computer Science Department, Colorado State University (1996)

76. Sklansky, J., Gonzalez, V.: Fast approximation of digitized curves. Pattern Recognition **12**, 327–331 (1980)

77. Spielman, S.: The logic of tests of significance. Philosophy of Science **41**(3), 211–226 (1974)

78. Stein, P.: A note on the volume of a simplex. The American Mathematical Monthly **73**(3), 299–301 (1966)

79. Stevens, K.A.: The visual interpretation of surface contours. Artificial Intelligence **17**, 47–73 (1981)

80. Subramanian, K., Barrow, J.D.: Alignments of clustered quasars. Monthly Notices of the Royal Astronomical Society **218**, 587–592 (1986)

81. Turing, A.M.: On computable numbers, with an application to the Entscheidungsproblem. Proceedings of the London Mathematical Society **2**(42), 230–265 (1936). Correction ibid. 43, pp. 544–546 (1937)

82. Ullman, S.: The Interpretation of Visual Motion. The MIT Press (1979)

83. Wagemans, J.: Perceptual use of nonaccidental properties. Canadian Journal of Psychology **46**(2), 236–279 (1992)

84. Wall, K., Danielsson, P.E.: A fast sequential method for polygonal approximation of digitized curves. Computer Vision, Graphics, and Image Processing **28**, 220–227 (1984)

85. Witkin, A.P.: Intensity-based edge classification. Proceedings of the National Conference on Artificial Intelligence pp. 36–41 (1982)

86. Witkin, A.P.: Scale-space filtering. IEEE International Conference on Acoustics, Speech, and Signal Processing **9**, 150–153 (1984)

87. Witkin, A.P., Tenenbaum, J.M.: On the role of structure in vision. In: J. Beck, B. Hope, A. Rosenfeld (eds.) Human and Machine Vision, pp. 481–543. Academic Press (1983)

88. Zhu, S.C.: Embedding Gestalt laws in Markov random fields. IEEE Transactions on Pattern Analysis and Machine Intelligence **21**(11), 1170–1187 (1999)